RAISING THE STAKES

The Modern Cricket Revolution

A Pitch in Both Camps

Jump Jockeys

Lambourn, Village of Racing

Fred, The Biography of Fred Winter

My Golf
(*with Ted Dexter*)

On the Rack
(*with David Gower*)

Lord Ted, The Dexter Enigma

RAISING THE STAKES

The Modern Cricket Revolution

Alan Lee

VICTOR GOLLANCZ

LONDON

First published in Great Britain 1996
by Victor Gollancz
An imprint of the Cassell Group
Wellington House, 125 Strand, London WC2R 0BB

A catalogue record for this book is
available from the British Library.

ISBN 0 575 06229 0

Typeset in Great Britain by
Rowland Phototypesetting Ltd
Bury St Edmunds, Suffolk
Printed in Great Britain by
St Edmundsbury Press Ltd
Bury St Edmunds, Suffolk

Contents

Introduction

In October 1995, Steve Waugh, the Australian Test player, was batting for his state side, New South Wales, in Perth when he hit a six against a sponsor's sign on the scoreboard. This fleetingly amusing yet apparently inconsequential incident was in fact something of a defining moment in the hectic development of the cricketing lifestyle. Through a publicity stunt dreamed up by the company concerned, Waugh had qualified for a substantial windfall: that one hit earned him £70,000. When interviewed on his stroke of good fortune, Waugh cheerfully admitted that he had not deliberately set out to hit the golden egg. 'I don't think anybody would,' he said, then paused before adding: 'Well, possibly, Don Bradman could have done.'

But Bradman would not have had the chance. In his day, over half a century earlier, cricket was not a commercial marketplace for the players to shop in. There were no such fortunes to be won on the swing of a bat and the arc of a ball. There were no sponsors' signs – indeed, there were no sponsors. Neither were there any of the other trappings of the game in which Waugh-of-the-1990s was playing. Bradman did not wear coloured clothes, or a helmet, or sunglasses, or designer footwear. He did not play under floodlights. All of these things would have been inconceivable in his day. As inconceivable, perhaps, as players wearing sponsored wristwatches, carrying briefcases and mobile phones to keep in touch with their agents, and driving sponsored cars as soon as they were capable of signing a professional contract. As inconceivable as umpires in orange shirts and daily fitness sessions of the type, in Bradman's day, that were deemed appropriate for military purposes only. As inconceivable as one-day cricket.

The end of Bradman's career coincided, neatly enough, with the end of the first half of the twentieth century. The player who completes his career half a century on – Graham Gooch, say – will have experienced a different game entirely. And what of the young men starting out as the millennium approaches, those, like Dominic Cork, who are making the headlines in the 1990s? Their generation finds it difficult to relate even to the likes of Gooch, let alone to a generation earlier: the men such as Raymond Illingworth who began playing their cricket in the 1950s.

In that distant era, cricketers in England had a measured lifestyle, if a poorly rewarded one. They played solely three-day games, starting on Wednesdays and Saturdays. Sundays were free for charity games, or golf, or time with the family – a rare privilege for the player of today. Motorways were a thing of the future, cars were a luxury for most cricketers and county teams travelled the country, often by contorted rail journeys, in a make-do style. Hotels were two-star at best; the evenings consisted of drinking beer, eating at steakhouses and talking cricket, usually as a team unit. The county circuit was undemanding, fitness levels poor and general expectations of success – in Yorkshire and Surrey apart – depressingly low. The amateurs left the game, but their legacy remained.

The fortysomethings of today, those who started playing in the 1970s, were the children of the revolution. Limited-overs cricket had arrived, to be greeted without great enthusiasm or understanding by the players yet, initially at least, revitalizing the domestic programme, restoring crowd appeal and raising the profile of the player. Expectations lifted in unison as money became, for the first time, a significant incentive rather than simply a cause for grousing. A few, elite players began to earn substantial sums and to be tempted by more. These players lived through the Kerry Packer years and came to know their worth, to aspire to greater things. Steak bars, keg bitter and begging a lift were consigned gratefully to the bad old days.

And now, in the 1990s, the new wave of cricketers is different again. Distinctly different. The game they play and the speed at which they live bear no comparison with cricket and the lives of cricketers of the 1950s and have little in common even with the 1970s. Everything is faster, more demanding, more scrutinized by the media and more preyed upon by the less scrupulous of the money men. Cricket is now a game in which the good will be comfortable and the great will be rich, but it is not necessarily a better game for that. Players are physically fitter but technical standards have dropped. There is too much cricket, leisure time is at a premium and, to a degree that can and will be argued among the generations, the joy and characterization has gone from the game. The modern cricketer, depending on your viewpoint, is pampered, helmeted and either utterly anonymous or glamorous, athletic and marketable.

The game they play is incontestably distinct from that played by their recent predecessors, so much so that to compare players from different generations becomes increasingly futile. The modern cricketer is just not playing the same game. In the 1990s, the leading cricketer is burdened with absurd schedules, dictated by commercial and political concerns but seldom, if ever, by the welfare of the player himself or by any interest in the longevity of his career. The peak of one-day cricket, at county level, is long past but the trough has been mismanaged, the need for cutbacks regarded with cowardly diffidence.

All this, of course, works to the detriment of the cricketer who has to turn up and play. He is not, however, a pauper by any means. Even as an uncapped second-team player in a modern shire side he is likely to drive a sponsored car, stay in comfortable hotels and enjoy a social parity with the senior capped players, even the internationals, that would have been anathema when Raymond Illingworth first played for York-shire. The nineties is the age of the wine bar, the clothing contract and the syndicated newspaper column.

And yet, for all the stark differences, there are as many similarities between the generations. The 1952 edition of *Wisden* lamented: 'Many players are cricket-weary and travel-tired before August arrives. We should prune the competitive programme or players should be rested in turn, as they are when on tour. The modern cricketer will relate whole-heartedly to such sentiments. In 1974, *Wisden* reflected on the season in which Graham Gooch, a painfully shy 'Mod' from Leytonstone, made his debut for Essex and concluded that the County Championship was in need of reform. 'For years,' the good book pronounced, 'over-emphasis on defence has been a characteristic of England's Test and county cricket. Hence, the decline of interest in the championship.' Seventeen years later, when a Staffordshire boy named Dominic Cork brought his brash, modern ways and his hero-worship of Ian Botham into the Derbyshire dressing room, *Wisden* returned to this familiar theme, proposing that the County Championship should be split into two divisions to create more intense com-petition, while at the same time bemoaning playing standards and 'fatalistic attitudes'.

The 1951 County Championship was won by Warwick-shire, and *Wisden* reported: 'There were no stars in the Warwickshire team – none of their men was chosen for Eng-land.' Two generations on, the same county were winning the championship again, and the same anomaly was applied. Plus ça change . . .

The concerns of the early 1950s about the declining appeal of cricket were expressed loud and long, and not without reason. Compared with the championship cricket of today, in which the vast majority of games produce a positive result, there was a preponderance of colourless, moribund play. Fifty per cent of championship games were drawn, a trend which provided a rare farce during a match at Trent Bridge when, in perfect batting conditions, Glamorgan scored 12 runs from 15 overs, so enraging the opposition that Reg Simpson, the Nottinghamshire captain, brought himself on and bowled a series of mocking lobs to his counterpart, Wilf Wooller.

Such shenanigans were an insult to the paying public, so it was small wonder that the then secretary of MCC, Colonel Rait Kerr, wrote an impassioned article on the need for more enterprise in county cricket. He was privy to the balance sheets of the first-class counties and they made increasingly grim reading. Cricket had been complacent in the post-war boom, smug in its traditional ability to attract patrons. But times had changed, and alternative leisure distractions were making their mark.

As the game finally awoke to the existence of competition, a fascinating table was published showing the rise in popularity of interests that could be considered rivals to cricket. In the first half of the twentieth century, the number of tennis clubs in the country had risen from 320 to 5,300, golf clubs from 120 to 2,100 and ice rinks from 2 to 52. Additionally, in 1951, there were 5.2 million cars on the road, indicating that motoring was a passion for rather more of the population than had been the case at the turn of the century, when there were only 4,300. It was also the era of the cinema, of which there were 5,700. Cricket, plainly, no longer commanded the automatic attention of the leisure-seeking populace. But compare this with the distractions available as the century draws to an end.

Not only have sports such as tennis and golf claimed an ever-increasing share of the leisure market, but the youngsters of the 1990s are also being seduced by entertainments of the technological age undreamed of by their counterparts two generations earlier. Satellite television, video, computer and laser games flood the marketplace, requiring any sport that wishes to compete to ensure its modernity, its commercial viability, in a way that traditionalists will inevitably find vulgar.

So the player of the millennium will dress, play and live utterly differently from his predecessors. He is being swept along on a tide of change so irresistible that no one can accurately forecast where it will ultimately take the game and its protagonists, though some say it will be to paradise and others to purgatory. The modern player is aware of his image, of his 'market value'. Whether he is as aware of the danger of overkill shortening his career or of the risk that he is more remote from his public than his predecessors is less certain. But he is not going to change; the game has taken him too far and too fast along a newly built trunk road for that.

Back in the anxious 1950s, a poem appeared in *Punch* magazine, its subject the torpid pace of the national summer game. The following is an extract:

> Cricket is slow,
> Thank God for that, when fever drives the mind
> Through burning miles we leave more miles behind
> To build new hells and let the beauty go . . .

But the game could not stand still, or it would die. *The Times* sensed as much and produced an ingenious, if prejudiced suggestion that the left-handed batsman should be banned 'because he interferes with bustle'. Thankfully, the game's administrators paid no heed to this, but they did, at their own measured pace – too slow for some – respond to the changing times – and too radically for others. And, like it or not, they must keep responding, or they will lose their players to a satellite game run by entrepreneurs of predatory instinct. In the 1950s, cricket was standing still. Two generations on, it is travelling too fast for its own health.

1

The Cricketing Apprenticeship

Almost a century ago, in the summer of 1898, Herbert Strud-wick joined the staff of Surrey County Cricket Club and reported for work at Kennington Oval. He was to do so most days of each summer for the next sixty years, first as a player held in great affection and high esteem (he played twenty-eight Tests for England) and latterly as the club scorer. Few men have served a county club for longer or with such distinction. This placed Strudwick in a singularly suitable position to pass comment on the way the game had altered in his time.

Writing in the 1958 *Wisden*, Strudwick reminisced about the time when he started out in the county game. He concluded:

> The young professional of today has a much easier time than when I began, of that I am sure . . . My first wage was £1 a week – no match fees – for four months during the summer, (plus) expenses, train fare and 2s 6d a day for lunch. Tea was free, and how we enjoyed it. If we could not get lunch on the ground we went to a pub, for there was always one close by. There, we had either arrowroot biscuit and cheese or a large piece of bread and cheese. That cost 9d or 1s, so we made 1s 6d on our lunch allowance, which was then quite a lot of money.

Strudwick's prudent housekeeping would appeal to Raymond Illingworth, who has the Yorkshireman's abiding belief that a penny saved is better than a penny spent, but it is doubtful if the rest of his description would find such favour. Things were a shade more civilized by the time Illingworth made the trip from Pudsey to Headingley to join the Yorkshire staff. At least, the players were not expected to queue for bread and cheese in a nearby pub on match days.

Illingworth would contend, however, that in other ways the player's lot had not improved greatly at all – not at Yorkshire, anyway. He first played for the county side in 1951, on special release from the RAF, and until 1955 he did not receive a proper salary, it being Yorkshire's policy to restrict uncapped players to match money. If they did not play, they did not earn. 'There was no security at all,' complained Illingworth, who went on to make the financial rights of players a priority throughout his time as a county and Test captain and, more recently, as chairman of England selectors and team manager.

Despite being a regular member of the Yorkshire side from 1953, Illingworth had to issue an ultimatum to the county committee before he was capped and given a contract. By then, he had received an offer (which, as an uncontracted player, he was entitled to consider) from Warwickshire, who were prepared to pay him a basic £850 a year plus expenses. It sounds a pittance now, but, as Illingworth reflects, 'All I was getting at the time was £8 for every home game and £16 when we played away. Out of that I had to meet my own travel expenses and pay for my dinner. I needed a lot of help from my parents even to get by.' And so, in 1955, he approached the club captain, Norman Yardley, and asked him to tell the committee that he would leave unless he was capped. His wish was granted the following week, and he signed a contract worth £1,000, which put him in a slightly more fortunate position than one of his contemporaries: Doug Padgett, whose loyalty to Yorkshire is so boundless that he remains there today as club coach, made his debut in the same season as Illingworth, 1951, and he was not capped until 1958.

The Yorkshire policy was unusually demanding, but does it compare unfavourably with the contrasting haste of modern county clubs to shower their valued young players with caps, contracts and subsidiary perks? If Illingworth was made to wait too long for acknowledgement that he was appreciated by his employers, there is an alternative argument that his counterpart of today is a spoiled young man, offered too much too soon so that he has no realistic assessment of his worth but, instead, the dangerous complacency of assumed security.

It was a different environment that Graham Gooch entered two decades later. Essex, unlike Yorkshire, had never won anything and nor, until the 1970s, were they expected to. Although based within easy commuting distance of London, they were a small-time club, provincial in their ways. All this was to alter, of course, but when Gooch, at twenty years old, signed a two-year contract worth £1,075 a year, there was a rustic amiability to the club that did not remotely resemble the atmosphere at Yorkshire.

Gooch was a rarity then, as he would be now, in that he had shelved his cricketing ambitions for as long as it took to get some alternative qualifications behind him. Essex would have signed him significantly earlier, for his reputation as a destroyer of club bowling for Ilford in the Essex League was quite awesome, but Graham listened to the exhortations of his parents, Alf and Rose. In later years, they were to become the most faithful travelling mascots to his cricketing exploits, but when Graham left school Alf and Rose encouraged him to complete a four-year course in toolmaking before signing on with Essex. There is a case for believing that more aspiring cricketers ought to follow this course to safeguard their futures, but circumstances do not encourage it. County clubs nowadays are in serious competition for the services of any promising teenager and it takes a particularly channelled and self-possessed individual to resist the blandishments on offer to pursue your boyhood dreams. Gooch has never needed his toolmaking skills, but others who joined county clubs around the same time, and fell quickly by the wayside once their limitations of ability or temperament were exposed, might have given much for such qualifications as an alternative to the dole queue. The fallout in professional cricket is heavy and it is unlikely to decline in the coming years. The players' union, the Professional Cricketers' Association, recognizes this and is now developing a system of close-season degree courses for players. It is too little and too late for many casualties, but it is progress nonetheless.

Bob Willis was one player who rejected the advice of his parents and plunged into a cricket career. At nineteen he had played a couple of Second XI games for Surrey, before spending the following winter working as a petrol-pump attendant. His parents were suspicious of the insecurities of cricket and Bob was strongly urged to take up a desk job. He found the thought repellent, and when Surrey offered him a season's trial in 1969, he ignored family pressures and accepted it. 'I was paid £12 10s a week and I felt like a millionaire,' he recalls.

For someone who, like Gooch, was to go on to captain England, Willis initially earned derisory wages. After taking a winter job in the sanctions department at Harrods – a concession to parental wishes – he signed a one-year contract with Surrey, worth only £425, for the following season. By the end of that year he was playing for England in Australia, his gamble vindicated. Others, less talented and certainly less dedicated, have gambled and lost, and with a frequency not lost on those Hampshire players whose reaction to the arrival of the gifted young South African Barry Richards in 1968 was apparently none too welcoming. In his autobiography, written ten years later when his county career had come to a sad and unfulfilled end, Richards related how the resentment to his starting salary – a relatively generous £1,300 – was shown. 'In the indoor nets, the senior players sat like judge and jury watching Butch White, Hampshire's fastest bowler, test me out with an assortment of hostility. Somehow, my salary had become common knowledge and certainly some more experienced members of the staff begrudged a better wage than their own being given to a twenty-year-old with no Test career.' Richards subsequently won over the majority of his team-mates by weight of runs, if not at the time by charm of personality, but his experience is symptomatic of the jealous vigilance that becomes an obsession among county players when it comes to the cutting of the wages cake.

Willis had long since retired and Gooch was about to become England captain when Dominic Cork signed for Derbyshire in 1988. He was not yet seventeen but had already played minor counties cricket for Staffordshire, his home county, and Derbyshire were pretty convinced they had snared a teenager of rare talent. They paid him £2,400 and gave him a two-year contract. These days, he earns more than that in one Test match. One of Derbyshire's favourite sons, Bob Taylor, had been retired for three years by the time Cork joined the county. His had ultimately been a career of fulfilment, for although he had waited a long time in the shadows of the great Alan Knott to demonstrate his silky wicket-keeping skills on the highest platform, he eventually became an automatic choice for seven years, and played fifty-seven Test matches. He was an unimpeachable character, a role model supreme, yet, as we shall see later, there were facets of cricket, and characteristics of its players, for which he had nothing but contempt.

But Taylor, I guess, would wish to change little about the time he played his cricket or the memories it afforded him. He still speaks with a perverse fondness of arriving at the Racecourse Ground, Derbyshire's headquarters, in the spring of 1961 to sign his first contract, a three-year deal worth £350 per season. His father was with him as he approached the strange and unlovely structures that make up the home of the club and they headed, reasonably enough, for the grandstand building, assuming that the county offices would be housed within. Instead, they were to discover that this decrepit relic of a long-closed racecourse was owned and inhabited by the Ministry of Agriculture. The cricket office, to which father and son Taylor were redirected, was a dark and poky broom cupboard at the rear of an adjoining building. Taylor was not deterred, either by this or by his subsequent introduction to the Dickensian facilities for players at Derby. There was, he found, 'paint peeling off the dressing-room walls, bird droppings tumbling through the ceiling of the indoor nets, showers fitfully functioning and a toilet in our dressing room that gave off an appalling odour.' But Taylor, like most aspiring professional cricketers of the 1950s and 1960s, neither sought nor expected opulent surroundings. The squalor in which he began his long and distinguished career did not irritate or offend him until much later, when he had experienced better and become aware of how backward the game he had joined was. 'It was many years before I became embarrassed by the set-up at Derby,' he recalls.

County cricket has never been a route to riches, although in the immediate pre-war years, when only 12 per cent of the working population was earning more than £250 a year, the capped cricketer was included in that narrow, elite band. It was only right, of course, that a player who had proved himself over a long period should earn substantially more than the uncapped cricketer, who was still essentially on trial, and yet, down the years, to an extent that is only now being aggressively addressed, the meagre wages on offer for the novice county cricketer have been an active disincentive to those of a mind to play the game professionally. It is not possible to gauge how much talent has been lost through this dreary advertisement for the insecurities of such a life, but if the parents of Bob Willis, and to some degree those of Graham Gooch, are an indicator, it is a significant amount. Willis and Gooch knew beyond doubt what they wanted to do and, time has told, had the talent and dedication to carry it through. Others, perhaps equally gifted but slightly less focused on the possible goals beyond the paltry pay, peeling paint and subservience that was the young player's lot until the latter years of this century, will undoubtedly have been more easily dissuaded.

Human nature dictates that any professional person will make jealous comparisons between his lifestyle and that of someone better rewarded. It is the 'grass-is-always-greener' syndrome. Yet the comparisons made by cricketers with their equals in other sports have often been valid and usually depressing.

When, in 1995, Warwickshire won the County Championship for the second successive year, Dermot Reeve, their inspirational and innovative captain, was asked about the bonuses that would be coming the way of the players who had now won six major trophies in twenty-four months. Reeve was neither dismissive of the amount of money he would earn nor churlish about his employers – indeed, he made a point of saying that the club was 'generous'. But he could not resist a mischievous aside. 'Last year,' he said, 'my bonus was worth about two days of David Platt's salary.'

Dominic Cork makes a similar allusion. He was the meteor of English cricket in 1995 and if his 8 wickets in the Lord's Test win over West Indies did not guarantee him a new status, then his hat-trick at Old Trafford certainly did. He was not grousing; he wanted to stress, in fact, that he had never complained about the money he had earned from cricket – not even the £2,400 starting salary in 1988 that was, by then, pitifully below the average for an uncapped cricketer, let alone a skilled young sportsman. But he was bewildered, he confessed, by the telephone-number salaries being paid to footballers who, in many cases, had achieved nothing comparable with his deeds on an international stage. 'You see Stan Collymore on £15,000 a week at Liverpool and wonder why,' said Cork, shaking his head. His incredulity was understandable: at the time, Collymore was not even in the Liverpool side, let alone playing for England.

'Cricket,' Cork went on, 'is an underpaid sport.' It was a blanket comment, made to illustrate the disparity in earnings between equals in different team games, and if the more public examples of inequality are at the highest level, where Blackburn's Alan Shearer's declared profits of almost £500,000 in 1994 dwarfed the earning power of any and every cricketer, the area of greater concern has been among the lower rungs of each sport. Back in 1931, when Sir Stanley Matthews joined Stoke City, he earned only £1 a week. Legend though he was, he never did have a seat on the gravy train that soccer stardom was to become. Football clubs nowadays pay their young apprentices tolerably well, however, and it was an overdue concession to cricket's untenably dated salary system when, in the summer of 1995, the Professional Cricketers' Association won a 27 per cent increase in the minimum wage for both capped and uncapped players. This deal was significant for the lowest and newest cricketers. The capped players, in most cases, were already earning more than the revised minimum. The same did not apply to the newcomers.

There are other, less material signs that cricket is on more enlightened and informal terms with its impressionable young players than was once the case. A new recruit to a county side is no longer put through a year or more of initiation by the senior players, which in some cases amounted to taking a vow of silence and acting as general fag to the old hands. Dominic Cork, for instance, seems genuinely startled that such practices ever occurred, for he experienced no such thing. 'I felt I was one of the lads even when I first started out at Derby as a YTS player,' he reflects. 'I was always encouraged and spoken to by the seniors. I never felt there was anything of the "them and us" about it.'

Not everyone, however, agrees that this shift to modernity, acknowledging and encouraging the young rather than making them learn by mute subservience, is a desirable development. A theme that recurs throughout this comparison of the generations is the suspicion of some, predominantly older players and former players, that the young cricketers of today receive too much, too soon. This applies as much to social equality as to the more material rewards of the professional sportsman. The dressing rooms of the majority of county clubs have gradually become more democratic places, where the voices of the young and inexperienced can make themselves heard as much or even more than those of seniority and accomplishment. But does such democracy encourage a respect for the game and its traditions? There are those who think not.

Perhaps surprisingly, Raymond Illingworth is not among those who feel a return to old values is needed, though perhaps that is because he played for Yorkshire at a time when their senior players barely tolerated the young and did nothing to encourage any spreading of wings. 'It was a case of "Sit in the corner and speak when you are spoken to,"' he recalls, without enthusiasm. Consequently, while Illingworth is a believer in standards and traditions, his own experiences have convinced him that elitism of this nature can be damagingly overdone.

> The reason we didn't win the championship more often in the 1950s was our poor team spirit. We had the ability to remain the best team in the country but we just weren't together as a side. There was always more fighting than fun at Yorkshire, and it wasn't confined to making the junior players feel small. The seniors were at it among themselves, too. I especially remember a row between Brian Close

and Johnny Wardle during a game against Kent at Dover. Closey threatened to take Wardle round the back of the pavilion – and he was a former army boxing champion. But that kind of thing went on regularly.

Illingworth's personal grouse, never forgotten or forgiven, concerns the treatment he received from John Wardle, whose undoubted ability was offset by an implacable temperament that led, finally, to his acrimonious departure from the club. Illingworth suggests that the unattractive side of senior professionalism was particularly noticeable when a catch was dropped. 'I once dropped a catch on the boundary with a crowd of ten thousand or so watching and shouting derisively. As a young player, still making my way, the lapse made me feel sick. I felt I had been punished enough and the bowler in question only added to the pain I felt when, at the end of the over, he came across and openly rebuked me.' A hard school indeed, but according to Illingworth, this was no isolated loss of temper, more a routine reaction. Wardle, it seems, inspired utter dread in the junior ranks. 'I probably dropped eight or nine out of ten chances in 1953 and 1954, simply because I was scared to death of being shouted at by Johnny.' Being the character he is, Illingworth finally tackled the problem head on by telling Wardle precisely what he had done to a young man's confidence. By then, however, the damage was done.

Deference to seniority was still expected in the 1960s and 1970s. Bob Taylor, casting back to his formative months at Derby, recalls: 'A young player spoke only when asked. He was expected to listen and to take in the cricketing knowledge that was being passed around. I called the senior players "Mr" and all the juniors had to knock on the dressing-room door before entering.' A few years on, when that most durable and popular of cricketers, John Lever, made his debut for Essex, little had changed.

The old them-and-us attitude between the senior players and the younger ones was still not too far away, but I never found it quite as pronounced as I might have done if I had started at Lord's, for instance. I am not saying there was anything wrong with that, but we certainly did have to serve a tougher apprenticeship than youngsters do today. Even at Essex, the junior players had to know their place, and I must admit I was scared stiff in the early weeks. I just sat in the corner and didn't dare say two words to anyone.

Taylor and Lever, 'Chat' and 'J.K.' to their innumerable friends in the game, were each to play for two decades, becoming spokesmen as well as ambassadors for their profession. They witnessed many changes but did not resent the disciplines in which they began the game, instead doubting the latitude that was to prevail in later years. Graham Gooch, who came into a jokey and largely informal Essex dressing room in 1973 but was still expected to know his place, shares such concerns and believes strongly that the 1990s young professional would benefit from the need to show greater respect.

Gooch was so shy when he began his prolonged and distinguished Essex career that it was probably due to his own nervousness, rather than the rituals of initiation, that he hardly spoke. Keith Fletcher, who had just taken on the county captaincy from the hectoring but much-loved figure of Brian 'Tonker' Taylor, believes that if Gooch had played for a different county, one with stuffier ways and fewer comedians, he might have remained introvert and become morose. Certainly, it took him a considerable time to shed the boyish awe in which he held senior members of his own and opposing teams. He made his maiden century in 1974, against a Leicestershire side captained by Illingworth, in a dashing innings that carried Essex to victory after Illingworth, the old fox, had set them a stern target of 240 in a little over three hours. But it is said that even amid such personal and team achievement, Gooch exhibited his overt deference. When he hit the great Australian fast bowler, Garth McKenzie, over long-on for six, he walked down the pitch and apologized for his temerity.

Essex eventually brought Gooch out of his shell, though not before he had become aware and appreciative of a pecking order.

> You had to respect the senior players. There was still a distinction in those days – not boot-cleaning, nothing servile, because I had come in after all that, but the older players let you know they had been around a long time and I don't think it was a bad thing. There is less of it now, more's the pity. Young players waltz into the dressing room and think they are the business after a couple of games. There is no learning process, as there used to be, and very little of the old-fashioned respect. I remember a lad called Chris Gladwin coming into our side at Essex and immediately nicknaming Kenny McEwan 'Spam-head'. Now, Kenny might have lost a bit of hair, but he was a very experienced and accomplished player. If he hadn't also been such a nice guy he could easily have taken offence at this boy arriving in the dressing room and thinking he was on equal terms.

Is Gooch being reactionary, betraying his age? Or is there a valid point in his belief that cricketers who grow up without respect for their seniors are likely to grow up lacking respect for the game itself? Do the ways of the late 1990s, in which novice players expect and receive a dressing-room voice as soon as they have signed their name on a contract, mean that the young no longer listen to their elders and learn from them?

Does this contribute to the evident truism that the players of today discuss the game between themselves far less than was once the case, and are consequently short on the 'knowledge'?

What is undoubtedly a positive aspect of the more relaxed atmosphere prevalent today is the resultant disappearance of the element of intimidation and fear from the cricketing apprenticeship. It may have slipped too far towards another extreme, one where it is considered soft, old-fashioned and therefore unacceptably demeaning to be deferential, even overtly respectful, to older players, whose opinions and anecdotes are regarded with impatience, scepticism or outright scorn rather than the attentive reverence they once commanded. This is to be regretted. But the loss of the more stifling aspects of dressing-room protocol, those that belittled, retarded and in some cases probably destroyed sensitive young players, can only be thought progressive.

The dressing room has undergone a revolution and, in most clubs, it has been a relatively recent one. Until the last decade or so, informality was still widely discouraged, hence the experience of Greg Chappell, who arrived in Taunton in 1969, an aspiring, ambitious but as yet unaccomplished nineteen-year-old from Australia. It came naturally to him to address all those he encountered at the Somerset club by their first names; he never considered the alternative of calling them 'Mr'. Australians don't. But his familiarity offended some of the club's traditionalists and when he was overheard speaking to both the captain and the secretary without the expected formality, protests were lodged by members. Years later, when Chappell led his country with strength and dignity, those members may have looked back and concluded they had been a shade foolish. But then again, they probably did not.

We have come a very long way from the formative days of Herbert Strudwick's career, to be sure. In that article for the 1958 *Wisden*, he remembered the atmosphere that awaited a new recruit to the Surrey dressing room at the turn of the century.

> There was no ceremony about the arrival of a new member of the groundstaff. I received no introduction to the players, [I was] just told my duties and where to find the young players' room . . . there were two large rooms for the players, one upstairs for those who had played in the first and second teams, and the other downstairs for the rest. There were also separate doors to get on to the ground. I once went upstairs and ran into Tom Hayward [the club captain], who demanded: 'Who are you?' I told him and he said: 'You have the advantage of me and your place is downstairs.'

This 'upstairs, downstairs' mentality was consigned to history long before Dominic Cork signed his first contract with Derbyshire, and he was never restricted in terms of where he could go or what he could say. Far from it.

> I was always encouraged to talk to the seniors, to spend time with them. We had both John Wright and Michael Holding at the club as overseas players at the time and I remember speaking regularly with them, learning from them. That is surely how it should be. I agree that senior players should be respected, but you can take it too far so that it affects your cricket. If a young player is thrown suddenly into a first-class match he will not be doing his job properly if he is in awe of one or more of the opposition.
>
> I have grown up in the game believing that I can get anyone out, no matter what their reputation or record, and I would not be doing my job if I didn't.

That does not mean, for instance, that I have no respect for Graham Gooch, but if he is up the other end when I come on to bowl I don't stop to consider how many hundreds he made in Test Cricket. I had the ultimate example of this in my second game for Derbyshire. As a boy, I had always hero-worshipped Ian Botham and now, here I was, bowling at Worcester, taking two wickets with successive balls and seeing my idol walk in on a hat-trick. What do I do? Give him a nice half-volley? Of course not. I tried to get him out.

Cork is an impressive example of the thoroughly modern cricketer, the type who has been brought up on open government in dressing rooms and does not regard a young player starting out as a slave. It sounds very laudable, but if the worries of Gooch, among others, are proved correct, then the young players of tomorrow will not only be expecting high wages and lavish perks before they set foot in a county dressing room, they will also be demanding immediate rights in a way not far removed from anarchy. The traditional values and common-sense principles of the dressing room will be tested as never before.

2

Practice and Preparation

Barely a generation ago, cricketers scoffed at the notion of physical training. They got fit, or so they would insist, simply by playing the game, in the nets and on the field. Perhaps, when the game was uncomplicated by limited-overs demands and bewildering travel schedules, this really was sufficient. But it is not any more. Of all the changes in cricket in the past twenty years, the greatest revolution has been in the approach to fitness, both physical and mental. The modern cricketer is expected to contribute in all facets of the game, no matter what his primary role in the side. The rabbit batsmen at numbers 10 and 11 have dramatically diminished in number, much to the regret of many to whom their haplessness was both amusing and reassuring, a demonstration of professional fallibility, and the days when a fast bowler could graze at third man between spells, with the captain's permission to chase nothing that might inconvenience him, are long past.

When Bill Bowes died in 1987, his memory provoked anecdotes of an altogether different age, one in which it scarcely mattered what else a fast bowler was fit to accomplish, so long as he took wickets. Bowes, a kindly Yorkshireman with the look of a university professor, played fifteen times for England in the 1930s and, belying his academic appearance, had a hand in the infamous Bodyline attack devised by Douglas Jardine in

Australia in 1932–3. He continued playing for Yorkshire, with great distinction, for years afterwards and yet the scope of his duties was rigidly defined, as the obituary devoted to him in *Wisden* makes abundantly clear.

> When Bowes suggested that it might be a good thing if he were taught the rudiments of batting, he was told firmly that his job was to take wickets; he was not to waste his valuable strength on making runs. If he ever showed signs of forgetting this, his partners were expected to run him out. Similarly in the field. He was stationed at mid-on and, if the ball came to him, he was to catch it or stop it as the case might be. But if it passed him, he was not to move; it was someone else's duty to chase it and throw it in. This was fully understood in the Yorkshire side.

The idea of today's Yorkshire team approving a similar code for Darren Gough, a comparably valuable bowler, is patently absurd. For one thing, Gough would not stand for it, having been brought up to enjoy an involvement in batting and fielding as well. Yet Bowes was not alone in his privileges: it was common practice to protect the team's specialists from over-exertion, to conserve and channel their energies. Fielding, which today occupies so much of a professional team's preparation time and which influences results and provides its own athletic entertainment, was widely regarded as an imposition. Teams did not practise their fielding, at least not with the demanding, competitive routines devised for the modern players and most impressively displayed by the Australian sides of the past decade. But then neither did they undergo the training programmes, ostensibly unconnected with cricket skills, nowadays honed to a searching technical standard in the ceaseless quest to make players more mobile, resourceful and resistant to injury.

Alec Bedser is unimpressed by the new regimes, as all who are acquainted with him will be aware. Bedser was the archetypal English seam bowler in the decade immediately following the Second World War, strong as an ox, willing and able to bowl 30 or more overs a day and to walk several miles to a game carrying his kitbag. He would do his training in the nets, enough to carry out his duties on the field, and he was without question a master of his craft. Bedser stayed in the game, becoming chairman of the England selectors during the 1970s, but he remains scornful of the modern obsession with training, pointing out with a degree of validity that the bowlers of today are unfit far more frequently than he ever was. Bedser, however, was a singularly robust man, playing in an era when the demands on athleticism – as opposed to the energy and resilience required simply to bowl – were far lower than is now the case. Once again, comparisons are odious, but Bedser, who never tires of regaling an audience with reminiscences of how much fitter for cricket were the bowlers of his day, is right in that respect. However, if those bowlers, Bedser included, were transported to the 1990s and exposed to the different demands of a diversified game, they would have to adapt their preparation or perish.

Ironically, it was during Bedser's time as chairman of selectors that the England team began to show a greater awareness of fitness requirements, largely through the direction of a one-time international gymnast named Bernard Thomas. Officially, he was England's physiotherapist, but Bernard, now seventy but still running his private health centre just up the road from the Edgbaston ground, was very much more than that to the national side. Worldly, resourceful and diplomatic, he would become their 'Mr Fixit' on tour, always appearing to know precisely where and how to shop for anything from carpets to cameras, chaperoning the wives of players and tactfully emptying the England dressing room of the interlopers every tour produces. Oddly, for one whose life revolved around the game, he neither claimed nor showed any knowledge of or real interest in cricket, and there are those who feel that this was a drawback in his treatment of specialist cricketing fitness problems. But what Thomas did achieve, and was his legacy to the Test team when he stepped down from the role early in the 1980s, was a conviction among the players that they needed to do more than just bat, bowl and run a lap or two of the ground if they were to last the distance in a professional cricket career.

Ian Botham was nobody's idea of the most enthusiastic trainer, for his was a talent of instinct and flair, a triumph of bravado over bumptious disregard for the accepted disciplines of preparation. But in 1979, when his England career was still young and he was still impressionable, he offered a tribute to Thomas which was especially significant for its implication that the physiotherapist's methods were still a closed book to the great majority of workaday county professionals.

> Many people laugh at the training routine he [Thomas] puts us through on a Test match morning before play starts, but these work-outs are valuable. They get you supple, warm and co-ordinated, and the absence of strains and niggling injuries in the England squad proves the soundness of his methods. I wish every county side had the same attitude. As I travel around the county scene, I see spin bowlers with groin strains or fast bowlers with thigh trouble and I will ask them, 'Don't you do any exercises?' Often they reply, 'What exercises?'

Thomas handed over to Laurie Brown, once the bucket-and-sponge man for Manchester United, a successful convert to cricket who continues to work as physiotherapist to Lancashire. Dave Roberts took over from Brown and, in 1995, the job passed to Yorkshire's Wayne Morton. The necessary qualifications for the position may have increased over the years, and the methods of treatment and exercise routines may have subtly altered, but the need for such figures, capable of training the players physically, is now uncontested to the point where every county side has one. Their duties vary from club to club: some are restricted to traditional treatment of injuries, rehabilitation programmes and day-to-day exercises; others are set loose on whatever training routines they care to devise.

It is all a far cry from the customs of bygone days at county clubs. Raymond Illingworth points out that, until the mid-1970s, Yorkshire sides were required to do no more than turn up at the ground half an hour before the start of play, and even then the priorities during that period of preparation would generally be a cup of tea and, in some cases, a perusal of the *Sporting Life* before following the umpires on to the field. Hampshire teams under the legendary cavalier captaincy of Colin Ingleby-McKenzie were reputedly required to be in bed by ten, so that there was not too much time for sleep to intervene before play began at 11.30. And, trawling deeper into the archives of sometimes apocryphal but certainly symptomatic cricketing anecdotes, there are the tales of Denis Compton and Bill Edrich arriving for Middlesex games just in time to take the field, still clad in their evening wear from the revelries of the previous night.

Pre-season schedules were equally casual compared to the programmes of these enlightened times, when many counties take their playing staff overseas in search of an amenable climate, dry nets and competitive practice, while others impose a regime of training and 'bonding' – a term that would have meant nothing in the days of Compton, Bedser et al. – over a protracted period. In 1995, his single season as captain of Gloucestershire, Jack Russell brought all his players back for training at the beginning of March, a month earlier than is customary. The benefits were evident in greatly improved results, and Russell himself, so introspective a cricketer that many legitimately doubted his credentials to lead, was a revelation, attacking his duties in a gregarious way to which his players swiftly responded. Gloucestershire became one of the hardest-working sides in England.

Bob Taylor's career with Derbyshire spanned the evolution of training for cricketers. Thinking back to his initial days with the county in the early 1960s, he concludes that their idea of pre-season training 'would be an absolute joke to the modern player. In the first week it consisted of a couple of laps of running, then home at lunchtime. Over the next fortnight, we would have some running either side of lunch . . .' Taylor was still playing, to an impeccable standard, twenty years later, when the programme was somewhat different. 'Despite my advancing years, I was expected to keep up with the youngsters during pre-season training that resembled a commando course.'

Taylor, a neat man whose conscientious attitude to personal fitness was beyond reproach, grew increasingly scornful, late in his career, of the corner-cutting of the young. 'Too many seem to think that the game owes them a living and that they are doing us all a favour by turning out,' he once said. 'Too many of the younger generation want the rich pickings without doing the hard graft that qualifies them for such rewards.' Taylor was a strident critic of the ethos that swept Kerry Packer's piratical recruitment through the game in the late 1970s. He believed that the monetary rewards that became more readily available post-Packer turned the heads of a generation of young players and made many of them complacent. In 1985, the year in which he retired, he showed his concern by taking the unusual step of preparing a paper for all the young players at Derby, setting out what was expected of them in terms of attitude to net practice, standard of dress, diet, etc. It was a graphic mark of his frustration that such standards were, in his view, regressing after the advances made in the late 1970s, when the energetic and opinionated South

African Eddie Barlow came to Derbyshire as captain and reacted with an indignant, reformist zeal to the age-old but depressing customs of the county dressing room, which involved doing as little extra-curricular training as possible and applauding every onset of rain because it meant that the card schools could resume. Barlow was having none of that, and his enthusiasm, Taylor recalls, was infectious. 'We were the first county to start the keep-fit craze that all of us now take for granted. Soon all the counties were following us as we went through our stretching exercises before start of play – and even when it rained, Eddie ensured that the cards were kept out of sight while we pounded round the boundary.'

Derbyshire might have been among the leaders in the field, as Taylor claims, but their shift from the unquestioningly casual ways of old to the fitness obsessions of the thrusting modern cricket side was merely part of a trend around the country and through the cricketing world in general. No better example exists of the attention paid to fitness and its long-term benefits than the sustained pre-eminence of the West Indies through the 1980s and into the 1990s. Their passport to this uninterrupted and undisputed supremacy, achieved during a period in which international cricket itineraries became ever more cluttered, was the strength of their fast bowling. Opponents and romantics alike chuntered unhappily about the ethos of using an exclusively pace attack and there were times when it was numbingly one-dimensional to watch. But its success, at both Test and one-day level, depended upon the ability of the four fast bowlers picked at any one time to remain fit for their quota of upwards of 20 overs each day. To this end, the most influential move made by the West Indian side was the appointment of a rugged Australian named Dennis Waight as their team trainer and physiotherapist.

It seemed a crazy clash of cultures to place this brash man with a love of gregarious bar-stool banter in a dressing room peopled by proud and private black cricketers whose inclination – and in part also their motivation for playing the game well – was to do what no previous West Indian side had managed: to establish a superiority over the white nations who had invented the game and ruled it autocratically for so long. But somehow the unlikely liaison worked, and Waight became an indispensable aide to the West Indian players, a man on whom they relied for the fitness that was precious to them and in whom they trusted and confided.

Although, socially, they were poles apart, the beer-drinking Waight had much in common with the teetotal Bernard Thomas. He had not played cricket, and neither did he pretend to fully understand its complexities. Both men applied to the players in their care programmes designed to make cricketers more lithe and supple, and thereby better able to carry out their functions, rather than trying to teach them anything technical. And if Thomas created some interest when first he had the England side out doing physical jerks before a day's Test cricket, Waight's routines with the West Indies have, over the years, become a spectator attraction in their own right. Performed with an athletic precision by players who seem actively to enjoy the performance, and choreographed by the barking tones of this strutting, stocky Sydneysider, the sessions end with hugs and high-fives among cricketers who are naturally strong on bonding, more often than not to the accompaniment of a burst of spontaneous applause from the gathered crowd.

Fitness training, though now a generally accepted accessory to the cricketer's lifestyle, still of necessity means different things to different players. Take two recent England captains, David Gower and Graham Gooch. Both were enormously talented batsmen who consecutively earned pole position in the all-time list of England Test run-scorers, but their attitude to training was as different as their outlook on life. Gooch, a fretful, analytical and conservative man whose shafts of humour were for years exhibited only to those who knew him best, decided in the middle of his career that he was not fundamentally fit enough. His solution was typically wholehearted: he went to train with the footballers of West Ham United, and quickly began to aspire to their levels of fitness, and took up road-running with what developed into a passion. Gooch, heavy-boned and of shuffling gait, does not have the ideal body for an athlete, but as a result of his fanatical desire to remain the country's best player he developed sufficient stamina to run marathons competitively. To Gower, on the other hand, all this was complete anathema. Naturally fitter and more slender than Gooch, he despised running and had no great affinity with the gymnasium. As a captain, therefore, he did not ask many physical questions of his players, whereas Gooch – at least until frustrated by those of lesser self-motivation – felt that all should seek to attain their maximum levels of fitness.

There were similarly basic differences between Gooch and Gower when it came to net practice, and the attitudes they espoused themselves were, perhaps inevitably, those they passed on to their players during their respective years of Test captaincy. Gooch believed in practising every day; Gower considered nets were to be used only when a player felt the need. Gooch, who recruited first the England team manager, Micky Stewart, and then his friend and Essex team-mate Alan Lilley as a personal net bowler, was suspicious of free days and idleness, while Gower's relaxed approach to touring famously led to photographs in the tabloid press of him drinking and sunbathing on a yacht while his England side was suffering an embarrassing pre-Test defeat in the West Indies.

It would be simplistic and unhelpful to say that Gooch was right and Gower wrong, or vice versa. But Gooch's attitude is undoubtedly the more modern, while Gower, rare and wondrous talent that he was, sometimes gave the uncomfortable impression that his style would have been better suited to the 1950s, when doubtless he would have played as a distinguished amateur, practising precisely when he felt like it. It is difficult to imagine Ian Botham as an amateur, or even belonging to a gentler and less commercial age, but he too was an erratic netter and a very occasional road-runner. Although, like Gooch, he allied himself with a professional football club – in Botham's case, Scunthorpe United – his aim was to prove that he could play the game, rather than simply to improve his fitness. Botham and Gower were not, within these parameters, role models for the next generation, for they were among the very few able to fall back on talent and charisma when fitness failed them. And neither, strictly in these terms, were they good examples of the modern cricketer and his altered outlook to preparing himself for the game.

A far better example is provided by Dominic Cork. In 1995, Cork achieved more in the space of a few weeks than many cricketers manage in a lifetime, taking 7 wickets in an innings at Lord's, on his Test debut, and a hat-trick at Old Trafford two games later. It was the stuff of fantasies, yet it would almost certainly never have occurred had not Cork undergone a road-to-Damascus conversion two years earlier. Until then, his undoubted talent had been undermined by injuries and by his tendency to confuse acceptable aggression with overt, vocal hostility:

> I don't think I had ever taken my fitness seriously enough until it let me down a few times. When I suffered injuries to my knees and groin, I realized I had to do something about it. I started working harder on training programmes designed specifically for me, and it has certainly helped make me a better player. I don't resent the training at all, but I do only those things I feel are beneficial to my game. In general, cricketers in England are paying more attention to their fitness even than when I began, but there is still room for more, because there are

still too many unfit county cricketers who are wasting their ability to play at a higher level.

Cork no longer wastes his ability and, in South Africa during the winter of 1995–6, he was an important part of an England team that did not compromise on its fitness. As well as participating in the daily physical routines, many of the players – Cork included – went quietly and voluntarily to gymnasiums on non-playing days, or even after play. 'I worked with weights, did some aerobic training and used the bikes and running machines. It all helps to keep the fitness levels up early in a tour,' he says. Cork neither knew nor cared that the players of a generation or two earlier would have found such behaviour oddly excessive. But then, they might also have resented the imposition of pre-tour training camps at the National Sports Centre in Lilleshall, initiated by Ted Dexter in his time as chairman of selectors and made possible by the financial backing of Patrick Whittingdale, a city financier who just happened to prefer cricket to counting money. Part of his generous five-year sponsorship of the Test team's preparation was used to establish Lilleshall as a regular pre-tour base where players could restore fitness after the close-season break, work on technical aspects of their game with specialist coaches such as Geoffrey Boycott, John Snow and Alan Knott, and generally talk cricket together – a lost virtue of the last generation – to help engender team spirit. Some approached it with more enthusiasm than others, but very few denied its benefits.

If David Gower, as we have seen, chose a relaxed approach to physical preparation, he did not close his mind to innovation in other areas. While captaining Leicestershire, he was party to an experiment with a sports psychologist. To cricketers of bygone generations, up to and doubtless including Raymond Illingworth, psychology would have been derided as cranky and inappropriate, yet for present-day players it has become an acknowledged aid – not used or appreciated by all, it is fair to say, but no longer automatically regarded as suspicious. Leicestershire went to the Isle of Wight for their pre-season training in 1987 and had arranged in advance for a sports psychologist to attend. During the stay, many of the players submitted to hypnosis aimed at improving their self-belief. Jon Agnew, now the cricket correspondent of the BBC, allowed himself to be put under four times, enthused widely about the effects and determined to use the method again. Peter Willey, strong and silent and, unlike Agnew, not short of native self-confidence, was said to be intrigued by the principle but refused point-blank to be hypnotized himself.

One of the suggestions of the psychologist, whose relationship with the county was, as it transpired, only short-term, was that at critical points of a day's cricket Gower, the captain, should shout 'Shovel!' to his players, the aim being to create a communal feeling of 'shovelling' the pressure on to the opposition. Gower, who was disinclined to do much shouting in the field at the best of times, viewed this with a certain scepticism; quite what Alec Bedser and his peers would have made of it is probably unprintable. The point, however, is that here was an English county side experimenting with a new type of mental preparation, and one that other clubs have now pursued.

England's Test team has not, as a matter of routine, exposed players to psychology, although its exponents have been freely available to those who have felt the need of it. Mark Ramprakash, a gifted batsman whose prolific run-scoring for Middlesex was in no way reflected by the rigid, nervy failings of his stuttering Test career, voluntarily consulted the former Middlesex and England captain Mike Brearley, by this stage a qualified psychoanalyst. Ramprakash, however, was acting individually and it is highly doubtful that such a course of action would have been impressed upon him by the management of the England side. By contrast, within the South

African Test team, as in the politics of the country itself, there is a sense of fallen borders and open government. Bob Woolmer, the former Kent and England player who proceeded via a phenomenally successful period with Warwickshire into the job of coach to South Africa, has never been short of enthusiastic ideas and, in addition to psychology, he introduced a dietician, whose most publicized notion was to recommend the intake of jelly babies for energy.

Woolmer had expanded the territories normally explored by coaches with such success at Edgbaston that he should certainly have been offered a job at international level by England to prevent him from seeking fulfilment overseas. That no such offer was made was a commentary on the staid and stagnant nature of English cricket coaching, which for too long offered 'jobs to the boys' in the manner of English football, where management vacancies are habitually filled by shaking the kaleidoscope and identifying which of the familiar, failed contenders are currently out of work. Ossie Wheatley, the long-time chairman of the Test and County Cricket Board's influential cricket committee, said on leaving the post that one of his abiding frustrations was the refusal of the counties to accept and address the fact that standards of coaching were generally dire.

The role of the coach has altered, though, at least in some clubs, where man-management has come to be regarded as more of an off-field responsibility than the captain can be expected to deal with. Hence the introduction of team managers, directors of cricket and sundry other fancy titles. It has been pointed out with some force by a number of captains, Gooch and Mike Gatting among them, that the most successful county sides of the last twenty years have generally been those with a strong captain and a back-room, technical coach rather than those with a high-profile manager. And they are right. Whether this means that the days of the team manager are numbered remains to be seen. Many players enjoy having someone other than their captain, someone on the periphery of the team, to consult and to whom to tell their troubles. Others doubtless become confused about to whom precisely they are accountable when they play for a side which employs both captain and manager. This is a part of the evolution of the English game that remains inconclusive, a development that could still be reversed. It is impossible to feel the same way about much else in the methods of preparing players, now so different from their primitive origins of not so long ago that there are no boundaries, no stigmas, no prohibition.

3

The Games People Play

'A game is exactly what is made of it by the character of the men playing it. New laws, new ways of preparing wickets, new schemes of reckoning championships – these external things do not matter.'

Back in 1934, when Neville Cardus wrote these words, loyally romantic and dismissive of the game's perennially distracting debates, he probably had a case. England's domestic cricket was organized simply, for there was only the County Championship to be played for, and if its reckoning was not exactly straightforward – counties played anything from twenty-four to thirty-two games each year and the title was decided by each club's percentage of points gained against the maximum available – few seemed to worry overmuch. But it was not a system that could survive the onset of a more professional sporting outlook after the Second World War, and Cardus's assertion that the 'external things', the cosmetics of cricket, do not matter fell on increasingly deaf ears as the game's authorities tinkered relentlessly with the mechanics of their vehicle.

Raymond Illingworth came into a game in which each county played twenty-eight three-day games, a system he still considers the best and most symmetrical for the players, despite its transparently inequitable flaw: there were seventeen first-class counties, yet each of them played only twelve of their opponents twice in a season and the other four once each. When this was addressed, in 1960, the problem was merely deepened, unfathomably so: nine of the teams continued to play twenty-eight matches a year while the other eight played a full thirty-two. The championship was then decided on the total points obtained divided by the number of matches played. The one surprise about this absurdity is that it was allowed to pass muster for three years until, in 1963, the revolution rumbled into English cricket with the inaugural Gillette Cup and nothing was ever the same again.

By the time Graham Gooch arrived on his social-symbol motor scooter, the East End Mod setting out on a 1970s career with Essex, there were three limited-overs competitions. The John Player Sunday League (1969) and the Benson & Hedges Cup (1972) had been accommodated within an ever more complex programme as the counties sought to cash in on the popular appeal of the one-day game. The County Champion-ship was consequently reduced to twenty three-day matches, which meant there were now only four opposing counties that each club *did* play twice in a season. Although, superficially, everyone reassured each other that the championship was still the premier county competition, it was being dangerously downgraded in the priorities of the clubs, for whom financial salvation lay with a new audience – unsophisticated, largely uninformed, but out for a good time in the hit-and-giggle atmosphere of Sunday-afternoon cricket. They had come, liked what they saw, and stayed, though no one could be sure for how long.

There was a degree of soul-searching over the next genera-tion as it occurred to the more enlightened of cricket adminis-trators that the one-day game was not, after all, the panacea that some were happy to present and exploit it as. And yet when Dominic Cork signed for Derbyshire in 1988, the four competitions, biased three-to-one in favour of limited-overs cricket, remained the pattern for county players. The one significant change, introduced experimentally in 1988 and embraced fully in 1993, was four-day cricket in the County Championship, a belated recognition that reform and repair were necessary within a competition that had been allowed to decay, with depressing consequences for English playing standards. And so in 1993, for the first time, the championship was decided equitably, with each of the eighteen counties (Durham having joined the flock) playing the others once per season. Hallelujah. That it could have taken so long, so much of the game's history and so many insubstantial changes to arrive at what should surely be one of the pre-requisites of sporting competition – fairness – does not speak highly of the wit and wisdom of successive cricket administrations.

It would be comforting to imagine that this prolonged evolution of a playing structure was now complete, but of course it is not. No system is ideal, but the English arrangement still betrays too many imperfections. Some are obvious and uncontested, such as the patently absurd device of staging a 40-overs Sunday thrash between the third and fourth days of a first-class game, thankfully to be buried without honours following one last rendition of its folly in 1996. Others are more arguable, and argument there is aplenty. The root of much of it is money, and the reluctance of the club's accountancy-based 1990s committees to concede that the English game has suffered grievously for its voracious affair with limited-overs events and to admit that at least one competition and its philan-thropic sponsor should long ago have been dropped. The counties, most of whom came alarmingly close to bankruptcy in the years before sponsorship, are understandably reticent about killing off even one of the geese and their golden eggs but, in their obsession with financial prosperity, some of them have lost touch with the health of the game and its players. Hence, when the opportunity arose, in the spring of 1995, to acknowledge the overloading of the itinerary, the issue was shamefully ducked.

The Benson & Hedges Cup, played with a 55-overs-per-side span relevant to nothing else in the world and with its group stages scheduled for the three-sweater weeks of April and May, never did have any obvious place in the hearts of cricketers, nor even in the cricketing calendar, other than as a gratuitously additional tournament when the feeling about one-day cricket was unequivocally the-more-the-merrier. It has survived because counties, hiding behind the barely believable argument that 'our members like it', actually feel comfortable with a fourth chance of some silverware and, more pertinently, are loath to relinquish the annual pay cheque from the well-meaning, well-organized but utterly inappropriate cigarette company. It should not have survived beyond 1995, when the sponsor's contract was due for renewal, and it was to the great good fortune (unless one puts a more sinister interpretation on the timing) of the Test and County Cricket Board that they announced a five-year extension of the Benson & Hedges Cup on the very day that Keith Fletcher was dismissed as England's team manager. Fletcher, a well-liked character whose sacking was both unusually summary and dramatically unexpected, headlined the back-page news, and in places made the front pages, too, and even the broadsheet press could find space for only a cursory reference to a deplorable decision that could be justified only on financial grounds; the kind of decision made by treasurers rather than by cricket folk of foresight and integrity.

It was immensely ironic that Raymond Illingworth was facing the media at Lord's that afternoon, having accepted – against his initial instincts – an approach to combine the duties of England team manager with the role as chairman of selectors that he already filled. The Benson & Hedges issue was put to Illingworth and he diplomatically deflected it, at the same time leaving little reason to doubt that he was disappointed, if not surprised. Illingworth was long past being surprised by the ostriches of the TCCB, who purport to make decisions for the general good of the game but in fact make most of them for the short-term security of their own county clubs. Illingworth's first year as chairman, with its inherent obligations to attend various board committees, had been marked, he declared, by his 'banging my head against a brick wall until it hurt so much I had to stop'.

Things were different in his playing days. Not healthier, perhaps, for there were many counties outside the mainstream (represented, then, by Yorkshire, Lancashire, Surrey and Warwickshire) whose finances were greatly in need of the type of centrally distributed annual share-out which is now routinely made through the funds accruing from sponsorships and television rights. But if they were not prosperous times for the clubs they were simpler ones for the players, and Illingworth has no qualms about his preference for the old system.

> I'm pleased I played when I did. I don't even have to think about that question. We all knew where we stood and there was plenty of cricket for anyone who was any good. We played twenty-eight three-day games a season, starting on Wednesdays and Saturdays, with twelve points for a win and four for first-innings lead if you lost or drew. I still feel two three-day games a week was the ultimate, that it gave you a better chance as a youngster . . . but then, there were no distractions from one-day cricket in those days.

Illingworth the player enjoyed one-day cricket, perhaps because he was part of a successful county side, but also because the compressed personal duels and the need for captains to think on their toes appealed to him. He could see that it was here to stay and yet there was something impressively prophetic about a ruminative comment he made in 1969: 'The time could be approaching when we may have to consider one four-day match each week . . . and one full-day or half-day knock-out or league game.' Almost thirty years later he has not changed his views, and one half of his prediction did, latterly, come about. The other remains merely the fancy of the enlightened, to be constantly snuffed out by those of narrower vision to whom quantity is a dictating force.

None of this should suggest that one-day cricket has no value, nor that it is unappreciated. The Sunday League, sponsored in turn by John Player, Refuge Assurance and AXA Equity & Law, and surviving even a fallow, unsponsored year when the interest of television waned dangerously, may now have run its course, though many would argue vehemently against that view. What is incontestable is the impact it made on the game, the catchment it expanded and the effects – not altogether happy – it was to have on the approach and standards of the players who came into cricket knowing that Sunday was just another working day.

For the first eighteen years of his career, indeed throughout his time with Yorkshire, Illingworth's Sundays were his own. There were some charity and benefit matches, of course, but little that was compulsory and nothing competitive. If the Yorkshire team was playing an away game, Sunday might comprise a leisurely breakfast, a round of golf and a good lunch; during a home game it was possible to spend the day with the family, living, if only for that single day each week, a life of normality and stability that is beyond the English cricketer of today. All this ended with the introduction of the Sunday League in 1969, so it should come as no great surprise that the majority of cricketers greeted the new competition with a shortage of enthusiasm and affinity. It represented a threat to their accepted and jealously guarded lifestyle, something which any working person resents, and it also asked them to play a form of cricket that most considered too brief to be taken seriously.

The trivialization of the Sunday League, however, was not a nationwide response. Lancashire, who had an abundance of all-rounders (bits-and-pieces players, as they became known in the vernacular of later years) and some exceptional fielders, took immediately and hungrily to the 40-overs format, winning the sixteen-match, all-play-all league in both 1969 and 1970 and drawing huge crowds to their games. Like Sussex, earlier in the 1960s, Lancashire were an example of a moribund county revitalized by one-day cricket. In seven years, after the first, wary sampling of Sunday League cricket, they won six trophies and became renowned as the most formidable side in the limited-overs field. And this from a club which had suffered such heart-rending that the captaincy had changed five times during the 1960s. You would hear no complaints about the impositions and artificialities of the one-day game from this quarter.

Nor, to be fair, were many counties inclined to dispute the wisdom of the introduction of 'the Sunday slog' once they had realized that it possessed far greater potential for money-making than even its most ardent promoters had envisaged. Around the country, the games were attracting vast numbers of spectators, many of whom had never considered watching a cricket match before. They were drawn by the user-friendly playing hours, which began after lunch and ended in time for dinner (or, depending on how you spend your Sundays, began when the pubs closed and ended in time for their reopening). They were drawn by the guarantee of a result and the probability that it would be obtained by cricket of an adventurous nature, which bore no relation to the solemnities observed in the traditional first-class game. They were drawn by the unprecedented once-a-week accessibility of what most of them may have viewed as a complex and elitist pastime. The technicalities of pitch-reading, field placings, declarations and the unfathomable lbw law may have previously discouraged many from taking any serious interest in the game, but now they could turn up without worrying about their ignorance, for such deep matters were for the midweek aficionados. Sundays offered cricket for the people, in which the main object was, it seemed, to hit the ball out of the ground.

The acclaim for this simplistic version of the game was a triumph of hope over expectation and it brought welcome, sometimes essential funds into the county coffers. Those sides who found the game to their liking, such as Kent and Leicestershire, now under Illingworth, took on a jaunty new stride during the 1970s, so much so that Sundays became the highlight of the week for many within and connected with the clubs. Other counties, Middlesex and Northamptonshire prominent among them, could not come to terms with the brevity of the matches and their form in them did not reflect their accomplishments in 'proper cricket'. But even at these clubs, people turned up in numbers to watch their team being ritually beaten.

What those people neither knew or cared about, and what failed for many years to permeate the coaches and players of the counties, was the potential damage to techniques, and thereby to playing standards and to prospects at international level, that was resulting from Sunday cricket. Batsmen were being asked, indeed in some cases instructed, to modify their methods to cope with the defensive bowling and fielding that (as a barely noticed counterpoint to the applauded aggression) predominated on Sundays. This involved, most significantly, playing with an open-faced bat in order to 'work' the ball into the unguarded areas of the ground, which was often effective on a Sunday but invariably a recipe for cheap and ignominious dismissal if (as human nature increasingly dictated) repeated back amid the slips and gulleys of first-class cricket on a Monday.

On a Sunday, batsmen were to some degree expendable, their role as the gung-ho aggressors, and the consequently high casualty rate, being acknowledged by all; the bowlers, by contrast, needed to be irreproachable in their stinginess, discarding from their game all the native spunk and flair that may in cases have brought them hundreds of wickets and established their name. They were expected to adjust their length and line in Sunday cricket, where their duty was to restrict the score rather than to take wickets, and, understandably, many found it difficult to reapply themselves to the disciplines required when getting people out once more became the priority. The only area in which the Sunday League produced an across-the-board improvement in standards, as against a gradual erosion, was fielding, which developed to previously unexplored peaks as the saving of singles and turning of apparently certain fours into threes attained an exaggerated importance. This has had a beneficial knock-on effect at higher levels, even in Test cricket.

Yet whether, in another twenty years' time, the entire Sunday League saga will be deemed worthwhile must be open to doubt. It has ensured short-term financial enhancement for many of the counties and has given a previously uninterested section of the public a presumably expandable interest in cricket: so far so good. But do the detriments outweigh the benefits? Is the Sunday thrash ultimately responsible, more than any other single factor, for the undeniable fall in classical, technical application and, by consequence, in the stature of the England Test team? The answer is probably yes.

The Sunday League was not, of course, the first limited-overs competition, not by six years. The knock-out format that preceded it, initially as the Gillette Cup (by which many still stubbornly know it) and then, from 1981, as the NatWest Trophy, was greeted by a similarly ambivalent response from the players. Most of them, captains included, believed it would be a strictly temporary experiment and did not even bother, at first, to adapt their tactics and field placings from those they habitually employed in the championship. Hence the stories of teams obstinately or blithely deploying two slips and a gulley at the stage of a cup game where run-saving was paramount. It came hard, this obligation to defend, and it was strangely at odds with the hyperbole of the one-day game, the dash and the bravado.

Yet within a few years the Knock-out Cup (stabilized at 60 overs per side after an initial stab at 65) had attained a secure position in the programme: well within its first decade it had truly become the FA Cup of cricket, and it continues to hold such rank. The game is long enough to encourage some genuine, protracted duels and whereas the vast majority of one-day cricket around the world is now of 50 overs' duration, the Gillette/NatWest offers a more authentic, less hurried test of ability. Nobody to whom I have spoken – players, administrators or media – questions the right of this competition to be retained as the premier one-day event.

The switch to four-day cricket in the championship polarized the game. There were those who promoted the change for years beforehand and there were others still doggedly, philosophically opposed to the idea even after the rubber-stamping of 'A Blueprint for the First-Class Game', the 1992 report of the structure working party headed by the chairman of Middlesex, Mike Murray. Now, it had long been a habit of the counties who make up the Test and County Cricket Board to set up such working parties as a convenient device for delaying any sensitive decisions, and then to ignore their subsequent reports. That this one was treated differently was both a triumph for the conscientious Murray and a coded confession that the county game was once more in need of revitalization. This time it had risked its credibility through a demeaning of the three-day championship to a point where the cricket therein was soft and uncompetitive. The consequences at the higher level of Test cricket can only be a matter of guesswork, but it is certainly the case that England's pattern of form around this time betrayed the very same shortage of tenacity and resolution that was rampant in the first-class county arena.

Three-day cricket was no longer sustainable because too many clubs, perhaps even the majority, played it to an insulting formula which involved Team A attaining its batting bonus points on the first day and Team B doing the same on the second, before a captains' conference, maybe over a couple of pints or, less sociably, in the car park on the second evening, settled upon an equation of runs and overs that would comprise Team B's last-afternoon target. Invariably, it would prove necessary for Team B to offer up some dross (known as joke bowling) on the final morning in order that Team A should proceed without fuss to the agreed declaration. It was a sick, sorry and all-too-regular farce.

Of course, not every championship match was conducted so fraudulently. There were times when one side was so far superior to the other that no collusion was considered; there were also times when the imperfections of a pitch, the fallibilities of one team or the heroics of another would produce a result by entirely genuine means. Indeed, there were some fine three-day games. But there were also far too many that asked little of their participants bar a degree of patience until a final three hours that, to all intents and purposes, resembled the second innings of a limited-overs game. This was not first-class cricket as it had been created, as it had always been intended. It was a joke.

The arguments against four-day championship cricket were largely fatuous. Some counties claimed that their members would not enjoy the slower pace of the games, which was presumptuous on two counts. First, it patronized proper cricket-watchers who would be certain to appreciate that they were seeing something more authentic for their subscription fee; secondly, it gave the utterly false impression that the championship drew crowds worth counting anyway. Long gone, sadly, were the days of which Illingworth still speaks fondly, when Headingley or Old Trafford or the Oval would be bursting at the seams for a 1950s championship fixture. In the eighties and nineties, only a small minority of the clubs – Essex most notable among them – attracted crowds of more than 2,000 for a day's first-class cricket. The pattern was the same around the world, reflecting a shift in customer preference towards the major international occasions and the big one-day games, and nothing was going to alter that significantly, one way or the other, if games were played over four days rather than three.

By 1992, the year in which the document which became known as the Murray Report was published, counties were playing twenty-two championship games a year, three four-day matches being scheduled at both the beginning and the end of the season with sixteen of three days in between. Some thought this a satisfactory arrangement. I thought it a botch. Murray's committee advocated a wholesale switch and the counties, not without reservations in certain cases, accepted their recommendation. The working party also proposed that the Sunday League should be a 50-overs competition and that the Benson & Hedges Cup should revert to a straight knock-out, abolishing the mindless, early-season group games. Both changes were adopted and yet, by 1994, they had been reversed. So much for the brave new world.

The four-day game was working, however, and even those who had openly expressed their concerns, such as Graham Gooch, were converted. 'It is a better game, giving time and scope for the better team to win without resorting to anything artificial,' he explained. And this was generally agreed. Teams had to readjust their sights, to learn how to approach this new animal, just as they had needed to adapt to limited-overs cricket. It took time, not least because of the cynical disregard for proper pitch standards displayed by a number of counties, but better cricket resulted.

That this did not immediately translate into improved

performances in the England Test side was not a complete surprise. There was never likely to be an overnight transformation just because county cricketers were now playing a form of the game that more closely equated to Test matches. But whenever England lose badly, as they did frequently in the early 1990s, the massive and avid media group following the team ritually demands an inquiry. In Australia, early in 1995, the demands were made not only by the media but by the England captain, Michael Atherton. During an impassioned speech following a tour on which England were arguably flattered to lose only 3−1, Atherton made a number of damning points about the English game that he was later to repeat, and expand upon at great length. His beliefs ran roughly as follows:

1. There are too many county players.

2. The talent is spread too thinly, so that our cricket 'lacks bite and intensity'.

3. There is too much county cricket. 'Players lose their edge, their sharpness, and so standards drop even further.'

4. There should be a two-division County Championship. 'It might produce a bit of elitism, but there is nothing wrong with that . . . fewer clubs would mean fiercer competition among players.'

Raymond Illingworth, Atherton's England chairman, soon to become team manager, agreed wholeheartedly, especially with point 4. He had been proposing a split championship for years and, as recently as the November 1994 meeting of the TCCB, had officially brought his suggestion to the counties' attention once again. The response was depressing, and Illingworth knew in his heart that it would be years before it was adopted, but he also knew that, like four-day cricket, its day would come. He drew unflattering comparisons of tone between the great Roses matches of the 1950s and contemporary county cricket. 'There was certainly more tension between the teams than exists today. The players didn't speak to each other very much, it was that competitive.' Nowadays, by inference, he considered the atmosphere altogether too obliging, a fault that could most potently be addressed by reducing the number of games, so prevalent from August onwards, that affect nothing bar the pride of one or both sides. There are those who say that pride should always be enough, but they underestimate the modern sportsman's desire for meaningful, material competition, the sort of competition that a two-division championship would bring.

Dominic Cork, the face of 1990s cricket, does not agree. But then he wouldn't, would he? Cork's county, Derbyshire, would, as he freely admits, 'almost certainly be placed in the second division. As a Test player, I don't want to be in a second division if all the best cricketers are in the first. But I also don't want to leave Derbyshire. So I have to think it's a bad idea.'

Cork takes a more objective view of the remainder of the county format and the clutter that comprises his season.

> I like one-day cricket. I get a buzz from it, from the big crowds, the television cameras and the special pressures of expectation. I'm not a man who likes to hide under a rock so the profile of the game appeals to me. But there is too much of it in England and it is hard to argue with the view that it is one reason for our decline at Test level. There has to be a balance between financial gain and what is good for the players. We must have fewer games because the season is just too hectic.

Cork is at more risk than most. His talent, emerging so swiftly and spectacularly on to the international stage, is an invitation for him to be overworked, and, during the early stages of the 1996 World Cup, the degeneration of his right knee was the plainest warning to all that too much is being asked of England's leading cricketers. But will anyone take note and act? Or will the blinkered desire to fill every available day with cricket, no matter how meaningless, continue to hold its damaging sway?

4

Trains and Boats and Planes . . . and Cars

It is not just the game of cricket itself, its rhythm and its tactics, that have altered beyond recognition in the second half of the century. Nor are the developments confined to the cosmetics, the appearance of the players and the grounds. Though these changes have been startling enough, there has also been a constant evolution in the mechanics of actually staging the matches, of how the players are gathered together at a venue. Travel has undergone a remarkable revolution, and this will doubtless continue. Who is to know what method of transport will be available to the professional sportsman in another twenty years? The private aircraft, that coveted possession of the richest Flat jockeys and golfers of the 1990s, may very well be obsolete, having given way to some hitherto unimaginable Tardis. However, the Frankie Dettoris and Greg Normans of the sporting world can be left to dream on about such inventions, for the exotica of the travel industry will probably continue to leave cricketers untouched. Theirs is not a sport of individuals commanding astronomical rewards but a team game of several days' duration, factors which dictate a more functional vehicle.

Transportation has, nonetheless, come a long way since the 1950s. Trains have been replaced by cars, and the occasional flirtation with coaches. The perceived importance of the car as a status symbol, rather than merely a means of getting around, has not been lost on the modern cricketer. He now expects, as part of his contractual entitlement, a vehicle for his personal use, usually daubed along its doors with his name and that of some friendly garage. Opinions differ as to the merit of this idea, and it is my assertion that the sponsored car, donated rather than earned, is one more mark of the complacent cricketer who demands the accessories of fame before he has done enough to be known by anyone outside his close family.

In terms of travel patterns, county cricket has for obvious geographical reasons developed independently of Test cricket. When our story begins, national teams undertook their tours by ship, voyages which, in some cases, doubled the length of time they were away from home. There must have been deprivations, there must have been homesickness and there must surely have been seasickness. Yet to ask most who sailed the seas en route to their Test cricket about their experiences is to bring forth a romantic tale of such comfort, indulgence and camaraderie that it is a wonder the players' wind and waistlines were in any shape for playing cricket at all when they rolled down the ramp to disembark at Cape Town or Fremantle.

Not that every team enjoyed such opulence, as the following extract from the rules of a 1930s Australian tour to England emphasizes. However, this was the Australian women's team and, at least in the thirties, they seemed to operate under somewhat more restricted conditions than their male counterparts: 'No member shall smoke, drink or gamble while on tour. While on board ship, no girl shall visit the top deck of the liner after dinner.' As this joylessness was accompanied by stern strictures regarding the need to be in bed by 10 p.m. and to rise in ample time for the daily physical drill at 7.15 a.m., the attractions of life on a luxury liner may have been slight for the women cricketers of Australia.

For almost forty years now, England teams have travelled overseas by plane, and speed and convenience have moved on apace. When Raymond Illingworth was first chosen for a tour, the 1959–60 trip to the Caribbean, the MCC party bound for Barbados first undertook a seventeen-hour flight to Bermuda, with a refuelling stop in Gander in Newfoundland, and then transferred to a ship, the *Camito*, which cruised the islands via Guadeloupe and Grenada before docking at Bridgetown. Today, England teams board a plane at Gatwick Airport at 9.30 a.m. and are in their hotel rooms in Bridgetown nine hours later.

The 1962–3 Ashes tour party flew from London to Aden, where they stopped to spend a day with the British forces; proceeded by ship to Colombo, the venue for a one-day game to keep the joints loose and run off a little of the excessive dining; and finally reboarded ship for the leg to Fremantle, Western Australia. It was a tortuous – if, for many, enjoyable – way to begin a tour, the formalities of which would now-adays take about eighteen hours on a one-stop Jumbo to Perth. Illingworth is not slow to point out that the financial inducements for that lengthy winter away from home, hearth and his close-season job as a travelling representative for a greetings-card and fireworks company were not huge. 'We drew the series but our bonus was a hundred quid,' he says. 'And mine was cut by half for some disciplinary matter that I still don't understand today.'

Illingworth can, and often will, quote similarly unhappy figures about the cost of running a car in the 1960s, the era in which county cricketers began to use them on more than the rarest of occasions. No sponsored cars in those days, of course, as he will remind any who ask. And there were certainly none available in the immediate pre-war years, when the steady increase in the number of vehicles on the road corresponded with an alarming rise in accidents. In 1934, more than 7,300 people were killed on the roads, and the view that this was an era of reckless, devil-may-care driving behind the wheels of what amounted to new toys is borne out within cricket. Several county players were killed on the roads, the most famous among them Ted McDonald, the Tasmanian who played for Lancashire until the age of forty and who was described by Neville Cardus as 'a satanic bowler, menacing but princely'. In the anxious aftermath of such tragedies, a number of county committees took a firm line, forbidding their players from travelling to games in motor cars. Either side of the war, then, the train had to take the strain.

Yorkshire, as a result of their geographical location, had to do more travelling than most and, in the 1950s, it was their policy that the team should use trains for all journeys of more than 100 miles. 'On the whole, few of us minded this,' recalls Illingworth, whose skill at bridge was honed on the regular trips south to London. 'We played a lot, though some of the card games could get very competitive. One of the players once threw all the cards out of the train window during an argument over a hand.'

The Yorkshire players were well looked after. 'A lot of the journeys were of four hours or more and the guards got to know us well. We would have good restaurant seats reserved and the food on trains was a darned sight better than it is now. It was all quite civilized, once you were on board.' But it was the getting on board, the effort of marrying playing hours with train timetables, that often posed problems. 'There were times when we would finish a home game at Headingley, say, at six o'clock on a Tuesday and we'd have to dash straight to Leeds Station, still in our whites, to get on the 6.15 train to London for a new game on the Wednesday. Some of the homeward trains were not too convenient, either. If they didn't go through to Leeds, I would get off at Sheffield or York and Shirley [Raymond's wife] would have to get the car out to come and pick me up.'

As ever, amid the frustrations and diversions, there was

humour of a type best appreciated with the benefit of hindsight. Illingworth particularly remembers the onerous additional duties that travelling by rail placed upon the team's twelfth man and junior professional.

> The worst of the train problems always fell on them. It was an education. Say we were leaving Leeds for a match against Sussex at Hove. It would be down to the twelfth man, usually with the delegated help of the junior pro, to pick up all our kitbags at Head-ingley, put them in taxis to Leeds Station, tip the station guards to get them on board our train, get them off again at King's Cross and put them in taxis across London to Victoria, tip the guards again and get them on a train to Brighton, then load them on to one last taxi to get them from the station to the ground. What's more, the twelfth man had to fund all this himself and then try to get it back off the team when the game began. It wasn't always easy.
>
> It wasn't surprising, really, that the lads who had to do all this used to vent a few of their frustrations. Bob Appleyard was not greatly liked by the younger players and I remember one junior pro, no doubt worn out and fed up during one of these intermi-nable journeys, throwing his kitbag on to a train bound for Scotland when we were heading for Hove. Bob had to play in pumps.

Given the unreliability of modern trains, in terms of running to time, overcrowding and the stripping of old-fashioned ser-vices, it is inconceivable that county sides would ever return to such routines and almost as unthinkable that any self-respecting county player today would act as an out-of-pocket baggage master. Rather like boarding schools, national service and the obligation to bowl to pompous and unskilled members in the county nets, it may well have been thought a valuable part of the Academy of Life, but try telling that to the teenaged cricketer who is given a sponsored car before he has even played a first-class match.

Graham Gooch's first vehicle was not sponsored, and nor were his next three. The mauve scooter in which he made his first, eye-catching appearances at the Essex nets gave way, when he reached eighteen, to a decade-old Ford Prefect. 'Dad lent me the £60 I needed to buy it, as I was only earning £10 a week doing my toolmaking apprenticeship at the time.' He had graduated to an Austin Maxi when he joined Essex in 1974 and by the following summer he had a battered red Hillman Imp, in which he drove to Edgbaston for his startlingly premature and demoralizing Test debut. For his debuts in both the second and the first teams at Essex, however, Gooch relied on lifts from team-mates – of contrasting and revealing quality.

Gooch's first match in the Second XI was at Northampton. He remembers being taken under the wing of the experienced captain, Johnny Welch, who was essentially a club cricketer with enough ability, time and money to indulge himself at this reasonably exalted level. 'He picked me up at home in a Rolls-Royce Silver Cloud,' relates Gooch with wonder. Rather more down-to-earth was the lift he received from his Ilford clubmate and contemporary John Lever for his first-class debut at the Westcliff-on-Sea ground just outside Southend. 'J.K. had an old silver Vauxhall Victor. We were chugging along the A127 dual carriageway towards Southend when the engine blew up.' Once it had been established that the combined mechanical knowledge of Gooch and Lever would not restore the Vauxhall to the road that day, if ever, an anxious phone call was made to the Westcliff ground, where the young tyros were awaited. 'There were no team talks or exercise routines in those days, we just had to be there in time to play,' explained Gooch. 'But we were beginning to cut it fine and I was certainly worried that this was going to be the debut I never got to make.' Stuart Turner was dispatched from the ground to round up the strays. He searched the A127 in vain – by then they had accepted a ride from a taxi driver who was an Essex member.

When Gooch established himself in the side in 1974, his close friend and room-mate was the amiable South African batsman Kenny McEwan. It became a routine that instead of taking their own cars to away matches, Gooch and McEwan would drive the Essex kit van. Their role was, perhaps, only a short step away from that of the twelfth-man baggage master on the trains of the 1950s, and some of the journeys were no more comfortable. 'It was a Commer transit van, pretty decrepit, and it had a kitchen chair in the back in case we ever had to carry a third passenger. One day we were heading for Manchester when someone threw a brick through the windscreen. The van wasn't the quickest of movers anyway, but with a shattered screen we didn't reach the hotel until just before dawn.' Modestly, Gooch does not add that his bleary-eyed innings at Old Trafford later that morning was worth 94.

John Lever remembers another endless journey, another splintered windscreen. The Essex team was on the road from Swansea to Eastbourne, quite an undertaking at the best of times, and the Lever windscreen came to grief on the Severn Bridge. There was no convenient stopping-off point for repairs, nor much time to worry about it. 'We just had to keep going. There were some curious looks from the holiday-makers as four Essex players drove into Eastbourne on a balmy summer's evening huddled in sweaters, scarves, duffel coats and anything else warm we'd been able to find in the boot, yet still wearing sunglasses to protect our eyes.'

It was in the 1970s, when all three one-day competitions were underway and the fixtures computer at Lord's was evidently unable to accommodate them all satisfactorily, that the itineraries of the county cricketer became ever more absurd, ever more life-threatening. Raymond Illingworth, by now enjoying an Indian summer as captain of Leicestershire, recalls the 'crazy white-knuckle drives', mainly on Friday evenings, and sometimes having to direct teams from one end of the country to the other. Occasionally, the Sunday League game would also be an inconvenient distance from the concurrent championship fixture, so players could find themselves driving for several hours, in fading light and when physically exhausted, on Friday, Saturday and Sunday evenings. The only wonder was that the road-casualty statistics which so alarmed the county committees of the 1930s were not depressingly swelled by cricketers forty years later.

Barry Richards, who was to become so sadly disenchanted with the routines of county cricket, was given an early taste of its sour side. His first championship match for Hampshire, in 1968, was at Hove, where he made an unbeaten 53 in the second innings of a draw. The following morning, he had to strap on his pads again in Harrogate, north Yorkshire. 'We arrived at Harrogate at two o'clock in the morning,' he later recalled, 'only to find that no one could even get a nightcap. It was a temperance hotel.'

The stresses and risks of such journeys must have been obvious to all, yet it was many years before a more sensible county programme eased the situation. Four-day cricket was the greatest help in this and, quite apart from the direct benefits to playing standards of the longer, less contrived game, the peace of mind county players have gained from the reduction of unsociable travelling time is incalculable.

Some clubs have experimented with coach travel during the past twenty years. The general view is that it doesn't work for a team game which decants its players in a place for several days and, largely, encourages them to conduct an independent way of life. Having to rely on the remote possibility that ten other players might all want to do the same thing at the same time is a recipe for fractured team spirit. Graham Gooch's memory of an Essex coach journey to Scarborough for a Sunday League game, is explanation in itself of why it was the first and last the club ever made.

It was Derek Pringle's idea, but he caused most of the problems. First, when we set off on the Saturday afternoon, we couldn't find him at the agreed pick-up point just outside Cambridge. He was sheltering from the rain on a roundabout. Then he got out his *Good Beer Guide* and found an attractive place for a drink and some supper but the coach got stuck in a Yorkshire lane while we were looking for the pub. We never did find it, and nor did we get to the hotel in Scarborough until after closing time. But that wasn't the end of it. Somehow, Pringle's kit had got left behind so we had to scour the shops – or the few that were open on a Sunday – to find him some size twelve boots. To cap it all, the journey home, nose-to-tail in tourist traffic, was endless. I got to bed back home at four o'clock on Monday morning. Never again.

Bob Taylor has similarly bad memories of the 1976 season when the Derbyshire club, close to bankruptcy, experimented with the economy measure of coach travel. They were promised a luxury model but it turned out to be not quite what they expected. 'It was a disaster. The seats didn't recline, the television fell down off its raised area, we couldn't hear the stereo for the engine noise and it travelled at only forty miles an hour. Sometimes we were even overtaken uphill by cyclists. On journeys home from games, the drinkers wanted to stop at a pub but the teetotallers stayed on the coach, keen to get back on the road. Soon we were all sick of the sight of each other.' The coach went back to the coach company and the players gratefully returned to their cars.

It was 1978, by which time he had spent four seasons in the Essex side and played Test cricket for England, when Graham Gooch received his first sponsored car. It was not thrust upon him, either: he had to write around to the garages of his locality, offering his name. It was probably not the way he would have chosen to transact such business but, in the 1970s, few car dealers volunteered vehicles. Finally, Gooch received a positive reply from a Toyota dealer near Romford. He was to use and advertise their cars for the next sixteen years.

Perhaps it is small wonder, then, that Gooch feels the next generation have not had to earn their perks as he did. 'Some clubs now have a deal for twenty cars and not enough senior players to drive them,' he explains. 'So they give a seventeen-year-old newcomer a Rover. He hasn't done anything in the game but now thinks he has arrived, he's made it. It gives him illusions and false expectations. It's unhealthy.'

Dominic Cork does not wholly disagree. 'I had a sponsored car as soon as I had a playing contract,' he admits. 'I didn't think much about it, though I was quite pleased not to have my name on the side. But I do feel that sometimes players are given such things too early. They don't have to work at it and when their cricket is not going well they may be a shade too complacent to tackle the problem in the right way.'

Car sponsorships have their lighter side. In his chronicle of the 1988 season, *Eight Days a Week*, Jonathan Agnew related that the road skills of his Leicestershire team-mate Phillip DeFreitas fell a long way short of the on-field talents that had won him a number of Test caps. In short, he couldn't drive, and his repeated failure to pass his test was threatening the provision of a fleet of sponsored cars from a dealer who insisted that DeFreitas should be among the drivers. It was around this time that the Carphone group began involving itself in endorsements, and to cap it all, Agnew reported, DeFreitas was then offered an individual deal for a car and mobile phone. His solution was to return to his native island of Dominica and pass a driving test there. It was enough to earn him a licence, and to secure his perks, but not enough to avoid the barbs of Agnew's pen. 'One does not like to question the standard of driving in Dominica, except it seems the most common form of transport is still the mule and cart. Believe it or not, Phillip DeFreitas is now the proud owner of a fully sponsored Series 3, petrol-injected BMW. I just hope they both look as sleek in September.'

5

The Wisdom of the Bar

English cricket, by tradition, has always encompassed a social aspect, whether it is played on the rustic village green with its quintessential thatched pub or on the professional circuit amid the rigours and scrutiny of the first-class scene. Players like to mix, they like to buy each other a pint and they like to talk shop, to discuss cricket they have played and cricketers they have encountered. At least, they used to. The new-generation player no longer seeks to socialize with the opposition in the ritualistic way of his predecessors. He may not even socialize with his own side. Whether it is an outcome of overt professionalism, of a perceived requirement to appear focused at all times, or simply of a shift in social patterns that has diminished enthusiasm for the laddish, beer-swilling gatherings of old, there is less mixing, less communing over several pints of good ale and, most pertinently, less sharing of the game's latest wisdom, the equivalent of the London cabbies' 'knowledge'. Like most routines that have disappeared from the game, it is unlikely ever to be revived, and that is a shame.

There is no disputing this erosion of cricket's social chapter, and yet it has happened so gradually that the players of today may be scarcely aware that they behave any differently in this respect to those of a generation and more ago. And, if they are aware of it, it is a fair bet that they will contest the theory that their routine is in any way inferior. They can call distinguished witnesses for the defence, too. For some years, during his time as team manager of the England side, Micky Stewart belaboured the 'recreational' nature of our game, as compared to the more clinical way it is conducted overseas. Only in England, he protested, do young men play cricket as much for the social as for the competitive element. He was referring, of course, to cricket at club and village standard, but claiming that it had an unhelpful effect at higher levels where, by inference, he considered that there was little room for social niceties.

Michael Atherton, the current England captain, is of like mind. While he has never discouraged those of his players who wish to swap dressing rooms at the end of a match day for a convivial beer or two with the opposition, he is personally inclined to avoid it. In Australia, on the long and, for England, fruitless tour of 1994–5, Atherton did not share a drink with his rival skipper, the amiable Mark Taylor, until the day the series ended in Perth. Then, as if to make up for lost time, the two exhausted men drank together for several hours in the dressing-room area, swapping ideas and anecdotes from the winter's cricket. Atherton was to repeat extracts of this conversation many times in ensuing months, for he found it stimulating and instructive. As a gregarious man, he also enjoyed the sociability of the session, and found Taylor engaging company, but as a professional of singular focus, he was not about to change his chosen ways.

For Atherton, distance from the opposition is a necessity, an aid to his working methods. To orchestrate six hours of steely cricketing warfare and then to indulge in a session of matey backslapping before resuming hostilities the next morning is, he feels, a shade fraudulent. But for others, I suspect, the remoteness is born of something different, a shift away from the old enthusiasm for talking cricket and being a man among men. Dominic Cork makes no apologies for it.

I accept that players don't go to the pub and mix as much as they once did. I certainly don't, and I don't believe I'm missing anything through it. I actually dislike talking cricket at the end of the day. It just doesn't work for me. I like to get the game out of my mind so that I don't take it home and – if it's been a bad day – inflict the sulking on my wife. I want to feel mentally fresh in the morning and I choose to do that by thinking and talking about anything but cricket once play is over.

Is this the voice of the modern cricketer? Well, maybe, but not all of Cork's generation so readily accede to the new order. Angus Fraser, for instance, regrets the passing of the habitual close-of-play chinwag. 'When I started out with Middlesex, the whole team, and most of the opposition, would gather in the Tavern, or another pub close to Lord's, after most days of a home game. By last season, Mike Gatting and I were virtually the only ones left who looked in. I like nothing better than winding down with a drink and an undemanding chat about the game, so I quite miss the camaraderie of it.'

It is important here to draw a distinction between being sociable and being a personality. Nobody could justifiably dispute that Cork has brought a freshness of character to the game, and the same applies to Darren Gough. In an age of stolid anonymity here are two men, contemporaries and friends, who actively disprove the notion that the game no longer breeds characters. Merely because they choose not to follow the paths of their elders does not mean that they are lacking in charisma. What it may mean, however, is that the game's traditional well of off-field stories may be drying up as cricket's communal aspect decreases.

It is a world away from the long-gone days when the off-duty hours of a cricket team were conducted with unbending formality. Angus Fraser may pine for company over his evening pint, but he would not remotely identify with the rituals of the Middlesex side of the 1920s, when J. T. Hearne was the patriarchal senior professional there. Hearne, dapper and correct, was known as the Squire of Chalfont St Giles, and believed strongly that his tribe should follow a specific code of etiquette. His team-mate, Harry Lee, described a typical evening during Middlesex away games in his book *Forty Years of English Cricket*: 'J.T. set the hour for us to be at meals or in bed. When we came to sit down, the juniors stood back until the seniors had chosen their places. Then J.T. would take his seat at the head of the table and carve the joint, handing round the plates in proper order of seniority, and giving himself the carver's portion last of all.' Suggest such a stuffy scene to the Middlesex team of today and prepare for howls of laughter, doubtless followed by the remark that if Gatting, their current senior man, was doing the carving, then his legendary appetite would necessitate a substantial portion of the joint being held back until last.

Gatting himself is, as Fraser suggests, one of those who loves to talk cricket after play. He never seems to tire of it and frequently voices his despair of younger players whose conversation is directed, trivially but habitually, to any alternative topic. Gatting might possibly even approve of the practices of the 1930s Yorkshire side which won the County Championship seven times in nine years. They used to leave their promising youngsters no choice when it came to evening conversation, as indicated by the following extract from *Wisden*'s obituary of Bill Bowes.

He was taken in hand by the senior professionals and taught his trade with a thoroughness which does much to explain why for so many years the county was by and large the most formidable in the championship. Night after night, he and Verity, who started at the same time, were taken up to a hotel bedroom and the day's cricket was discussed, the field set out on the bed with toothbrushes, shaving tackle and the like, and praise and blame administered impartially as required.

Hotel bedrooms are seldom, if ever, put to such instructive use nowadays but they remain a constant topic of cricketers' conversation. More often, probably, than in any other sport, a cricketer's home is his hotel and the varying standards thereof are discussed as much as the life therein. The enforced routine can produce a false, insulated existence to which some players adapt better than others, and this is one aspect of the professional game that has not altered at all. Only the relative comforts and amenities have advanced.

Yorkshire followed a curious and diverse policy during the 1950s by leaving the booking of hotels for away trips to the players themselves. This inevitably created a class structure, with the senior professionals staying in one establishment, the juniors in another and sometimes the affluent amateurs in a third. The young Raymond Illingworth, thrust into this disunited system, stridently decries it.

Team spirit was never good at that time but it might have been considerably better if we had all stayed in the same place. At least some of the capped players might have made more effort to help the youngsters if they had shared the same breakfast table. We never met Len [Sir Leonard Hutton] for a drink at night and he never had much to say to us in the dressing room.

Inevitably, the senior players tended to stay in the better-class hotels while the rest of us congregated in cheaper places. We would play some silly games in the hotels – Brian Close would balance a glass of beer on his head as his party piece – but the young ones had to make their own entertainment and keep pretty much to themselves.

When we played at the Scarborough Festival each August, we had to stay up even though we were officially at home. It was too long and arduous a journey to do every day. The hotels were always full of holidaymakers and, when I started, I wouldn't know until the previous game whether or not I was needed. So we had an arrangement with a boarding house run by a Mrs Hoggs. She would agree to keep three or four rooms for us during the festival and, when we arrived, there would always be food spread out on a big table, covered by a cloth. Then we would sort out the rooms and, all too often, find there were more players than could comfortably be accommodated. I remember one year, Trueman, Leadbeater and Lowson had to share a double bed, though I don't think all three of them were in it together too often.

Fred Trueman stories from those days proliferate, and although in later life his tendency has been to indignantly refute any suggestion that he led anything other than a monk's existence, the evidence of those who played with him is somewhat at odds with such claims. Illingworth recalls how Trueman was forever oversleeping and how, on occasions, even his team-mates were unable to rouse him from his hotel bed. Already on a final warning from the club captain, Vic Wilson, he was sent home from Taunton one match-day morning in 1962 for arriving at the ground well after the toss. Trueman would have bridled and blustered at such treatment, but, in the long term, he would have remained completely unabashed. Just as, in more recent years, he has become an incorrigible bore when commentating on the game for BBC Radio, he had a predictable and repetitive subject matter in his playing days. Invariably, it was the quality and scandalous ill-fortune of his own bowling. 'To hear Fred talk,' said Illingworth, 'you would think he never bowled a straight one in his life. Everything was pitching leg and hitting off, or vice-versa.'

It would be easy to identify Darren Gough as the 1990s incarnation of Trueman: same background, same bowling style, same self-assurance. But Trueman's humour, or that involving him, at any rate, was largely characterized by amused exasperation at his boorish antics. Gough, while not a quiet or subtle man, offers a greater spontaneity. He pulls childish stunts in the dressing room, as Ian Botham before him was wont to do, but Botham, too, mischievously tended to pick upon those he knew were least prepared for his attentions. Gough's larks bring to many faces a smile of genuine appreciation. He spent the winter of 1994–5 in South Africa carefully repairing the damage inflicted by a demoralizing summer in which injuries, unsolicited advice and unreasonable expectations had conspired to diminish his self-confidence. Now he was part of a bubbly, young atmosphere, one in which he could once more express himself.

An opportunity arose one sleepy afternoon in Bloemfontein as a three-day match against the central South African province of Free State wound wearily towards stalemate. Gough, acting as twelfth man, had been upbraided by his team-mates earlier in the day for forgetting his duties at a drinks interval. When the last drinks break of the day arrived, he jauntily drove the electronic buggy to the middle and theatrically unloaded three bar stools, a television set and a stereo system for his team's indulgence. A few days later, as he bowled a fine spell without reward in the Second Test at Johannesburg, a plastic rubbish bag blew across the ground. Gough, walking back to his mark, picked it up and symbolically pulled it over his head.

These were the antics of a natural comic. They are rarely found in cricket – Gough's immediate predecessor in the Yorkshire side, Graham Stevenson, was another – and the game should be glad of them. But Gough had already discovered that, in the modern game, jokes are regarded as funny, as opposed to silly, only if they are accompanied by success. 'I shan't forget how certain people turned against me during my bad summer,' he said. 'They were the very same people who had said what a breath of fresh air I had brought to the game, and now here they were telling me I should learn to concentrate properly on my cricket.'

Gough was not the first to suffer the fickle strictures of those who believe it is only appropriate to smile when you are winning. Derek Randall, the rubber-limbed clown of the 1970s and 1980s, experienced similar problems with people who thought him hilarious one day and a pain in the backside the next. And doubtless, to some extent, the same applied to Ray East and sundry other comedians in the Essex side of the same era, though the difference here was that, most unusually, an entire team was caught up in a high-spirited atmosphere that seemed to aid their cricket. The captain – whether it was Brian 'Tonker' Taylor with his barking, military manner, or, latterly, the wry and deceptively resilient Keith Fletcher – would always be slightly above it all. But both privately savoured the spirit that was created around them – and why wouldn't they, when a club grown old as unquestioned also-rans suddenly began to sweep all before them in the county game?

These were heady days to be around the Essex team. On the field, they had learned to win, finishing off teams as only a side accustomed to it will do. Off the field, they were ungovernable, a side packed with characters who believed their lifestyle was there to be enjoyed. Not that they were all alike – far from it. Although there was the odd occasion when their evening social routines would coincide, there were some stark contrasts among them. After away matches they would invariably begin with a drink or two together, but then Fletcher and David Acfield, the learned and laconic off-spinner, would trawl the area for its best French or Italian restaurants and the next morning would look witheringly at what they called the 'scum-eaters' – the likes of East, Stuart Turner and Brian Hardie, whose culinary highspots were generally a burger joint or a hot-dog stall after numerous pints of beer.

Almost without exception, however, the morning would yield a fresh supply of stories from the previous evening's socializing. Almost all are unprintable here, but most were essentially harmless. Once or twice, the 'horseplay' brought recriminations, such as the incident in the early 1970s when Keith Boyce, the vivid West Indian all-rounder who was such a popular overseas player at Chelmsford, jumped on a hotel bed and broke it. It was past midnight when a salvage operation was launched and the team's most outrageous trio – East, Robin Hobbs and John Lever – carried the unusable bed down two flights of stairs and into a vacant room, where they swapped it with an undamaged bed which then completed the reverse journey. Their efforts were in vain, however, because the beds were of a different height and the switch was quickly discovered by hotel staff.

On another occasion, recalled by Graham Gooch, Essex were staying in an olde-worlde pub during a game at Wellingborough College in Northamptonshire. 'This place had a full-size knight in armour on show in the hall corridor and the manager was in a bit of a state when he came to serve breakfast and noticed that it had disappeared. Some of the boys had dragged it up the stairs, late at night, and tucked it up in bed . . .'

East, who possessed the social expressions of one born to be funny, was generally involved in everything, and his humour was not confined to social hours. A talented slow left-arm bowler who had a Test trial, he might have gone further but for the doubts in high places about his 'suitability' for the international stage. He was just too jokey, they said;

he didn't take the game seriously enough. And it was hard to disagree, for on occasions he could drive even his own captains to distraction. His funniest – or most irresponsible – moments were generally reserved for his batting, which was serviceable without being especially brave or consistent. One day at Portsmouth – a notoriously quick pitch – East infuriated Andy Roberts, who was then at the peak of his considerable powers, by not walking when he clearly gloved a catch to slip. An angry Roberts was a formidable foe and East did not like what he saw. In a cricketing equivalent of raising the white flag of surrender, he walked smartly away from his stumps as Roberts exploded into his delivery stride, gratefully allowing the next ball to bowl him.

Like most county sides – and even modern-day touring England sides – Essex players had to share rooms when they were away. Some cricketers find this claustrophobic and restricting but others are grateful for the company. Within the Essex team, some long-standing friendships were forged from the accepted pairings of Lever and Boyce, Gooch and McEwan, Hardie and Turner and, most surprisingly, East and Acfield. Different in almost every way bar their shared role as spin bowlers, these two quarrelled and bitched and insulted each other as a daily routine, yet somehow the partnership worked and they would have missed it had they been separated.

County sides, especially those with cramped budgets, did not always stay in hotels boasting more than one star in the 1970s. Gooch remembers one night before a NatWest Trophy fixture when their unromantic billet was the Newport Pagnell service area on the M1 motorway. 'When we got up in the morning we had to walk across the motorway footbridge to a Little Chef for breakfast.' These days, counties generally establish a favourable rate with one of the major chains and stay in their three- or four-star hotels whenever possible, although any player unfortunate enough to be demoted to the Second XI will notice a sharp decline in luxury.

At that level, pubs, bed-and-breakfasts and those depressing hotels that were once euphemistically advertised as being suitable for 'commercial travellers' (in one night, out the next morning and never mind the quality) remain the order of the day. For all that, it is a learning environment for the young and impressionable cricketer, off the field as much as on it. Bob Willis recalls his first game for the Surrey Second XI in 1968, an away match against Worcestershire at Evesham.

> We were due to go on to Glamorgan afterwards, so, although our meals were paid for, I was sent away with £5 from my father to cover the week's emergency expenses. My first night away was an eye-opening experience. After dinner, the senior guys played spoof in the bar. I had never played it before but, not wishing to be thought unsociable or unversed in the bar-room arts, I accepted their offer to join in. It goes without saying that I lost, discovering that the game involved more than mere luck, and to my horror the round of drinks I was obliged to buy amounted to £1 17s 6d. More than a third of my emergency money was gone and we had not even started the week's cricket.

One final Ray East story to sum up the Essex team and the 1970s cricketing culture. Essex were slated to play Warwickshire at Edgbaston and, travelling as usual in a scattered convoy of cars and vans, they arrived at their nominated hotel in Birmingham's long, noisy and anonymous Hagley Road. When John Lever parked his car and carried his bags into the lobby he discovered East already there, pacing the foyer fretfully. Aghast, he reported to Lever that the club had committed that most cardinal of sins: they had booked the players into a temperance hotel. As ever, the resourceful wise men of the side found an answer, darting out to an off-licence for a seven-pint pipkin of bitter, which was then placed in the washbasin of one of the rooms. 'We never stayed there again,' said Lever. 'We were already sleeping three or four in a room on some away trips, and a temperance hotel was just too much.'

Every team has its hotel horror stories, tales of the day they turned up and found no trace of a reservation, when the showers sprayed mucky brown water, the restaurant served inedible food, the bar refused to open. One of the most graphic illustrations of both the standards of accommodation and the crazy schedules that pertained a generation ago comes from the former Lancashire Trojan Jack Simmons. It dates back to 1969, when Lancashire were faced with the daunting drive from Swansea to Tunbridge Wells on a Friday night in June. The pretty Kent town was crowded due to the making of a film, and the Lancashire side had been shuffled into the annexe of their appointed hotel. Simmons relates: 'We arrived well after midnight and Graham Atkinson, my room-mate, pulled back the bedclothes to reveal cockroaches on the bed. The place was filthy and there was damp under the bed, too.' Atkinson and the club scorer, Mac Taylor, tucked their trousers into their socks and sat in chairs around the spartan table all night. Simmons, less squeamish, claims he stripped the bed, shook it and then slept on it. Somehow, they got through the night, though there were some bleary eyes in the dressing room the following morning as personal stories were ritually swapped. Unsurprisingly, the team had checked out of the rogue hotel at breakfast time but this move hardly made life more comfortable for them, for the vagaries of the fixture list had contrived to give them a Sunday League game at Peterborough, which involved another late-night arrival. Thereafter, they booked into a London hotel and commuted to Tunbridge Wells for the two remaining days of the championship game.

Life could be more fun than this, however. Provincial away

trips were generally anticipated with enthusiasm by the more sociable of county sides and while the ritual close-of-play pints would be sunk in the pubs attached, or adjacent to grounds (the Taverns at Lord's and the Oval, the Cricketers at Leicester and Hove and the Bat and Ball at Canterbury), stories also abound of parties in rural hotels. The Diglis, on the riverbank at Worcester, is now a stylish and sedate establishment, but in its earlier incarnation, prior to some years of in the wilderness decrepitude, it was the scene of some wild and wonderful nights when county teams of the 1960s and 1970s came to town.

It was in this era, in 1968 in fact, that Barry Richards began a career with Hampshire that was to bring him countless runs and countless admirers but, ultimately, disenchantment with his lot. He had joined a county well known only a few years earlier for its wild behaviour under the captaincy of Colin Ingleby-McKenzie. On his first away trip Richards became acquainted with their reputation. Hampshire were playing Sussex at Hove and Richards had been dismissed cheaply by John Snow. After the day's play, the team returned to their seafront hotel, the Imperial, a mile down the coast in Brighton. 'Quite how the transition took place from a couple of sorrow-drowning drinks to a corridor chase armed with lavatory brushes, I will never quite understand,' Richards pleaded later. But the frolics became ill tempered and the South African newcomer, who had a short fuse in those days, was sufficiently riled to kick out the panel of a door. Penitence came with the dawn, as it so often does, and the young Richards was grateful and surprised to find that the hotel manager hardly turned a hair when the damage was confessed. 'I later discovered that he was quite used to such a rumpus because a couple of years earlier, Colin Ingleby-McKenzie had wrought similar havoc on a door panel with a spear.'

A decade later, as he prepared to leave the county game, Richards no longer took any pleasure from the social side of his cricketing life. In fact he was thoroughly depressed by it, as he explained in his book *The Barry Richards Story*.

> The routine is interminable. Every match is a carbon copy of the last. You travel to away games, often on journeys that have more in common with a mystery tour than a drive to work. You reach the hotel. You book in. You go downstairs for a few drinks. You go out to a Berni Inn, you feed on steak and chips, you come back and you go to bed. You wake up in the morning. You have your breakfast. You read the papers. You have a cup of tea. You play the day's cricket. You have another drink. And you go back to the hotel and the routine starts again, day after day after day, ad nauseam ... By 1977 I had become so disenchanted that even a hundred before lunch left me with no sense of elation ... The ritual has left me totally numb and I know that when I walk off a county ground for the last time it will be with an enormous sense of relief.

The emptiness that Richards felt had more to do with his frustrated international aspirations than anything else. But for the isolation of South Africa he might have decorated the Test circuit for fifteen years and become acknowledged as one of its finest-ever batsmen. Instead he was left to fester in the backwaters, and fester he did. His bitterly expressed criticism of the county-cricket routine did not endear him to fellow professionals and, much later, he was to regret the way he had done things. Such awakening was a while in the coming, however, and when I interviewed him two years after his retirement, by which time he was working, bizarrely, as a van driver and public-relations agent for a freight company in Australia, he was unrepentant. 'I have not kept in touch,' he said. 'I haven't even looked at the scores. The reason I have not missed county cricket is that it was so predictable. This past summer, you could have told me the time on any one day and I would have told you what the Hampshire players were doing. The routine was stifling.'

Contrast this attitude with the boyish enthusiasm sustained by Jack Simmons, for whom retirement from county cricket was something to be resisted and postponed for as long as humanly possible. Granted, there was a difference in circumstances, for Simmons had come into the game late and without great expectations, but he also had a different outlook. When Lancashire signed him, as a twenty-seven-year-old Preston draughtsman, it was, he said, 'like a fairytale'. And when, many years later, a lucrative benefit completed, he remained as eager to play as ever, it irritated him to have his motives questioned. 'It disappointed me that people could even ask that,' he reflected. 'I still played because I enjoyed it.' Jack not only enjoyed the bowling, of which he continued to do plenty, but the team routines which Richards so openly despised: the close-of-play camaraderie and, in his case, the legendary quantities of fish and chips on the way home. But Simmons was a throwback; certainly, there are few of his like around now.

These days, the norm is represented more accurately by Dominic Cork, whose attitude is that cricket is for daytime hours only. He defends his social preferences staunchly, claiming, 'It may even be a more sophisticated form of players mixing. I still meet up with team-mates and friends among the opposition, but it tends to be done over dinner with our wives or girlfriends, rather than by drinking four or five pints in a pub.'

But Graham Gooch, among others, regrets the changing ways and sees within them a sad diminishing of some of the game's enduring values. By way of illustration, he goes back to his own formative years as a player and the away games he anticipated most keenly.

I used to love playing against Somerset at Taunton. Brian Close was their captain and he would hold court in the bar every evening. I could listen to his stories all night, because he made me laugh. But I learned from him, too.

Until very recently, we would always get changed at the end of a day and then have a drink or two with the opposition, either in a local pub or in a bar or sponsored box on the ground. Nowadays, quite suddenly, really, it hardly ever happens. The norm during away games for our guys is to go straight back to the hotel, and when we are playing at home, most of them just disappear.

Players no longer exchange views on the game at the end of the day, which was all part of my learning process. You built up a bank of knowledge about opponents, some of which was very useful, simply by comparing stories with other players. And because we no longer mix so much, we also don't get to know the game's new characters so well as we once did. It all contributes to the increased sense of anonymity about the modern game and I think it is very sad.

6

Parochial Power:
The Influence of the County Clubs

'Let any Whitsuntide only be reasonably fine and warm and a great multitude will march every morning on Old Trafford . . . man and boy, this crowd has been going to Old Trafford in Whit Week these fifty years; man and boy, it will be going there in thrice fifty years to come.'

Lyrical, rousing words, once again from Sir Neville Cardus, penned in the 1930s. They were hardly prophetic, though: the teeming crowds to which he referred had dispersed long before even one more half-century was complete, and not only from Old Trafford. Social habits and expectations had changed and cricket, along with other traditional sports and entertainments, could no longer take its audience for granted. There was no multitude waiting to march on the county grounds every bank holiday; there was no multitude in the county grounds at all. And, though Cardus may have erred towards rose-tinted romanticism in his confidence that future generations would view the game as he did, he had no way of knowing that the difference would be so acute, the desertion so complete.

Now, as the end of the century approaches, first-class county cricket in England is little different from the first-class state or provincial programmes elsewhere in a world increasingly obsessed by international competition. At domestic level, nobody goes to watch; or, at least, those who do are instantly recognizable as retired folk who have joined the county membership (a category that will diminish sharply as a generation passes on without leaving behind it a like-minded replacement), schoolboys on outings or the dottily devoted few known colloquially, and unkindly, as anoraks. Oh yes, there is one further group, though they scarcely qualify as spectators since so few of them actually watch the cricket. These are the corporate guests, those men in blazers invited by commercial companies which have hired a private box for a day or a match. They were not around in Cardus's time, for which he need not be profoundly regretful, but today it must reluctantly be admitted that it is they, not the loyal members and lifelong supporters, who provide the counties with their reliable day-by-day revenue. Cardus's 'great multitude', which conjures images of Lowry-esque figures clutching their sandwiches, drawn to the great Manchester ground purely by the lure of the game and its endless possibilities, has given way, around the country, to a new breed of cricket-attender – one who arrives in his company-owned BMW and finds a space reserved for him in a car park barred to the general public. He indulges in a day-long feeding frenzy that usually also involves copious quantities of drink and, almost invariably, the adoption of the classic corporate spectator's pose – back firmly pointed to the cricket – so that he will, in all probability, drive out of the gates late in the day with scant idea of score or details of the play. Nor, if the truth be known, any real interest.

It is a considerable sadness that it has come to this, that the game now has to pander to those who are not genuinely attracted by cricket at all, only by the social possibilities provided by someone else's expense account. But why has it happened? Is it simply the entertainment evolution, changes in the pattern of life and preferred lifestyles which could not be avoided and need not embarrass? Or is it a symptom of a malaise within the game itself, a development redolent of the self-centred complacency and mismanagement from which so many of our professional counties have suffered over a period of years? There is no definitive answer here, no incontestable right and wrong. But what is certain is that county cricket, and through it the English game in its entirety, has suffered grievously for being run by people who were either unwilling or unable to focus upon anything outside their own parochial orbit. They see their role in the game exclusively in relation to the short-term health and comfort of their own club and, if this conflicts with the requirement to sustain and nourish playing standards for the greater good, well, too bad. This is a generalization, of course, for there are, and always have been, some talented, visionary men involved at county level. But the fact that they have been in the minority, and that the small-town mentality has traditionally held sway, is as unarguable as it is disturbing.

In the 1990s, like it or not, all professional cricket must devote itself primarily to the needs of the national team, sometimes at the expense of long-standing local tradition. That this is being grasped only slowly by some of those paid to run the counties, those who remain intransigent in the face of overwhelming evidence and urgent need, is depressing, as a former chairman of the Test and County Cricket Board agrees. In February 1995, when England had lost yet another Ashes series even though it was barely past the halfway mark, Raman Subba Row wrote a letter to *The Times*. Its content, though generously applauded by those with the broader interests of cricket at heart, did not go down well within the coterie of reactionary county administrators whose instincts for self-perpetuation rebelled against an attack by a man who had once been one of their own. What Subba Row had to say was this:

Since finishing as TCCB chairman in 1990 I have felt obliged to refrain from commenting publicly on the state of English cricket despite the continuing poor performances of our national side. Now that my successor has himself retired, and in the light of the escalation of our troubles to the heights of Prime Minister's Question Time, I regard myself no longer bound by that convention.

However disappointed we all are by England's results in Australia this winter, it is, I think, unfair to place the main responsibility for the failures on the players themselves. They will be as sad as the rest of us and they will know that they simply have not been good enough on a tour encumbered by unprecedented injuries.

Two problems should have been addressed some years ago: first, to find and develop young players to go into the England team at the earliest opportunity and, second, to restructure our domestic programme to prepare our players properly for international cricket. Those problems are not insoluble – it needs a drastic structural reorganization, resulting in the parent running the subsidiaries and not vice versa as at present. Vested interests have blocked progressive thinking and those, both amateur and professional, who run our national game have found it all too easy to shelter under the no-change umbrella.

Ailing organizations don't mend themselves; normally a financial yardstick comes into play. Regrettably, in this case, expanding revenue from commercial sources is only exacerbating the problem. More and more cash is being distributed to fund more and more mediocrity as well as expensive overseas players. Someone must break into this vicious circle of mismanagement and create a new accountable structure. The need is all the greater when time has already run out.

Subba Row was not unanimously admired as chairman of the board, largely because his working methods were those of a business executive rather than a slave to committees. He was, and is, a man of instincts and initiative, and if he felt there was an area of his domain requiring urgent action, he would not be inclined to waste precious time on consultation. Inevitably, this brought him into conflict with county administrators, who were unused to being bypassed in this way and resented the precedents that were being set. Technically, right was on their side, for the English game is a democracy and Subba Row showed an occasional tendency towards a dictatorship. But the vision he displayed, and the boundless energy with which he pursued his missions in the game, were refreshingly vibrant within an administration too often bogged down in bureaucracy. He made his mistakes, though – the absurd award of a tour bonus to the ill-disciplined England players in Pakistan in 1987 being the most notorious of them – and because his head was raised permanently above the parapets of self-preservation, it was only a matter of time before the jealous reactionaries claimed their victim. That his elected successor was Frank Chamberlain, a mild-mannered man of such apparently introverted ways that he made not one memorable statement during his five years as chairman, spoke volumes for the preferences of the men beneath him. They regarded such a chairman, compliant and non-interventionist, as ideal.

The players' view of county administrators, both the full-time employees and the essentially honorary committee men, is inevitably coloured by material matters. A secretary who comes up with a fleet of sponsored cars for the team will be popular; a committee that cuts meal allowances for away trips will not. This has not changed over the years, and nor is it likely to in the foreseeable future. What has altered, and is continuing to evolve with some speed, is the sort of man employed by the counties and the scope of his duties therein.

Retired military men used to dominate the ranks of county secretaries. They were considered by the committees to be the 'right type' for a job that required an organized mind and an unquestioning deference to higher authority – viz. the committee. There were some outstanding successes, too, but as time went by the custom of appointing majors, captains and lieutenants fell increasingly out of step with the progressions of the game. Such men frequently failed to relate to the modern cricketer or, indeed, to the pace of modern cricket itself. Sometimes unfairly, military prefixes became synonymous with the frustrations of the enlightened, who recognized that sport was in a fast lane and that cricket, stuck in third gear, was being left trailing in its slipstream. And so, imperceptibly at first, the military influence diminished. Now it has all but disappeared, and with it the title of secretary.

By 1995, only five counties – Glamorgan, Kent, Middlesex, Sussex and Worcestershire – continued to call their principal administrator the 'secretary'. Most of the remaining thirteen counties referred to him as the 'chief executive', a few preferring 'general manager'. It could be argued that this was merely semantics, and in some cases so it was. At certain clubs, however, the subtle change of title signified a change of status, a recognition that county cricket could no longer exist along the chummy and unambitious lines of a weekend tennis club; that it was indeed a business that required a more dynamic form of day-to-day supervision. Hence the new breed of administrators, some of them unashamedly appointed for their industrial, marketing or public-relations acumen than for any background in cricket (or, thankfully, the military). This development has not been an unqualified success. Surrey's troubles in the mid-1990s bear testimony to the fact that the

creation of a business structure and the appointment of
innumerable executives in every field of responsibility is not,
in itself, the key to running a cricket club. The dismantling
of the Surrey hierarchy in 1995, which culminated in the
resignation of their high-profile chief executive, Glyn Wood-
man, was an emphatic demonstration of the failings of a club
that had lost sight of its priorities.

Simultaneously, there was a silent coup (the silence being
a rarity in these parts) at the Yorkshire club, which suddenly
had to find a new chairman of cricket, captain and coach. For
followers of the fortunes of the white rose, however, there
was nothing very unusual in this. Successive Yorkshire committees had indulged in internecine discord for generations,
and Raymond Illingworth was only one of many players who
have held the committee of their day in disregard:

> Between the players and the committee it was a case
> of them and us. There were more than thirty on
> the Yorkshire committee, including a lot of area
> representatives, and although ours was an unusually
> large county it just made for an unwieldy organiz-
> ation. There was a large cricket committee, whose
> duties included picking the team – but although they
> were selectors, three or four of them could recognize
> hardly any of the players. It's no wonder we had
> little respect for them.

The Yorkshire committee was not the only one to suffer this
accusation. Bob Willis, who began his county career with
Surrey in 1970, had a similar complaint. 'There was a lack of
any decent relationship between players and committee . . . It
was a standing joke that some of the committee did not know
the players even by sight, an allegation borne out at an end-of-
season party when one of their number approached Younis
Ahmed and asked, "Who are you?"'

Illingworth's disdain for those who ran his club, however, extended beyond their remoteness from the team.

> There was a meanness to the committee, too, that did not endear them to the players. In those days, it was something of a custom for the committee men of the home county to entertain the visiting players to drinks, maybe on the first evening of a championship game. It was a pleasant formality, a way of breaking the ice, but Yorkshire would never do it. Neither would they do anything to make opposing teams feel welcome by organizing golf for them on a Sunday, as often happened when we travelled away. This was an embarrassment to us, especially when we played Lancashire, whose committee was exceptionally hospitable. Typically, the first time that Yorkshire did lay on a drinks reception in the committee room, at Bramall Lane during the 1960s, only two of the committee bothered to turn up.

Lancashire may have been a hospitable club but this was no safeguard against strife. In the 1960s, as their team languished consistently in the lower half of the championship table and suffered increasingly by comparison with their neighbours and fierce rivals Yorkshire, the saga of unrest at Old Trafford was one of soap-opera intensity. They went through five captains in that decade, even plucking one, Joe Blackledge, from league cricket for a single season in charge, and on one famous occasion the club placed an advertisement for a new captain in the classified columns of *The Times*. In 1964, disgruntled members called a special meeting and threw out the committee, the ultimate sanction at a club where expectations of success were constant and unfulfilled.

Such a level of public demand was rare in county cricket

at that time. It had long existed at Yorkshire, although, as Illingworth recalls, 'The expectations of our members were huge. Basically, they expected us to win the championship every year and wanted to know what had gone wrong if we did not. They turned up to support – we would close the gates during a Roses match or when Surrey came to Headingley – but our standards had to remain high to satisfy them.'

This was not reflected elsewhere in the country, largely because most supporters were given no encouragement to believe their respective counties had any chance of winning the championship: Surrey won it seven years in succession between 1952 and 1958, and Yorkshire won it in seven of the next ten years. It was only in 1969, when Glamorgan astonished everyone by taking the championship for only the second time in their history, that an air of greater accessibility began to prevail, for this was also the year in which the Sunday League was launched, providing a second, season-long league for counties to target. It was the salvation of Lancashire, where peace broke out when the club won the John Player Trophy in each of its first two years. As the Sunday League became established, it also offered incentives to counties who had grown wearily accustomed to their role as also-rans. In eight years, between 1976 and 1983, the title was won by eight different counties. So, disregarding for the moment the argument that its style and brevity was causing untold damage to the techniques of English cricketers, the Sunday League was at least achieving one purpose: that of refocusing counties on the possibility of success. Indeed, when the advent of the Benson & Hedges Cup in 1972 increased the number of competitions to four, there was scarcely a county in England which did not start each season believing – some more realistically than others – that they were capable of winning one or other of them.

This was a double-edged sword, for as opportunities increased, so too did demand. Graham Gooch points out how different the Chelmsford ground is now from the place where he began his Essex career in the early 1970s. It is physically unrecognizable, for one thing. Chelmsford was primitive, as the 1974 *Wisden* reminds us – 'it is to be hoped that there will soon be a permanent scoreboard at Chelmsford in place of the portable affair that has served for so long' – but it is the difference in atmosphere that strikes Gooch.

> There was no expectation of winning when I started. We tried, but if we didn't win, we didn't win. Nobody lost their job over it, and nor did the members get annoyed. They simply weren't used to us winning, so they made no demands of us. The big difference now all comes down to money. To obtain the sponsorship all counties now need to survive and prosper, you must have success on the field. So there is a constant pressure on the players to produce results.

This pressure manifests itself in a variety of ways. The players know they will be substantially better off if they begin winning trophies, but their performances also reflect upon the club's administration. If a team is not winning, the modern instinct is to examine the input of the committee and, most prominently, that of the chief executive. Cricketing jobs are not protected by custom as once they were; the lifestyle of those working within the game, as well as those playing it, is immeasurably more precarious than it was a generation ago. And for one reason alone: success is no longer a distant ambition, it is a demand.

The demand comes from commercial sources, who want to see some recognizable return for their investment in a county. But it also comes from the members, who in the main are no longer content to offer mute and unquestioning compliance to the vagaries of their adopted clubs. Memberships have been rising in various counties, usually as a result of concerted efforts to attract new recruits, even at a vastly reduced annual subscription, and the profile of the typical member is not nearly so predictable as it was even a generation ago. The vocal ones, though, those who transmit their views to the secretary and pick up their pens to write letters of protest to national newspapers, do fall into a more coherent pattern. Essentially, the people who are passionate about a county are not the same as those who attend international cricket, and nor do they share the same priorities. Many county members, for instance, bridle at the very mention of reducing the amount of cricket played in a season. It matters to them not a jot that such a reduction might benefit playing standards and hence improve the performance of the England team. All that matters, all that rankles, is that they would consequently have fewer playing days for their money.

This was the intransigent attitude that confronted the cricket committee of the Test and County Cricket Board when, in the autumn of 1995, it reviewed the structure of the domestic game in England. There were many pleas and suggestions for them to consider, a good number involving the dropping or contracting of competitions. The resistance to any such pruning came from counties who feared short-term financial loss and members who resented any reduction in spectating opportunity. Only one reform of note was implemented: shifting the starting day of four-day championship games from Thursday to Wednesday. By definition, this meant that games would now be scheduled to end on a Saturday and protests were inevitable: matches finishing inside three days would deprive the majority of members of their Saturday cricket. The planners this time had their answer ready, and it was a good and significant one: make sure your pitches are of four-day quality and then games will generally run their course.

The standard of county pitches has been one of the ongoing scandals of the English game in the last generation, responsible as much as any other individual factor for the regression in batting and bowling excellence. Everybody knows it; there can be no argument about it. And yet, with a cynical disregard for the consequences, some counties continue to prepare (or under-prepare) pitches simply to guarantee a result. It is one more outcome of the change in expectation over the past thirty years; one more example of how the craving for success can be self-destructive in the long term.

Derbyshire, more than most, have been accused of manipulating their home surfaces to suit their predominantly seam-bowling attack. Somewhat disarmingly, their long-serving captain, Kim Barnett, has regularly admitted the charge and offered the defence that home advantage should be precisely that. It is a theme further explored by Dominic Cork, one Derbyshire bowler who has stood to gain from such pitches.

> We have pitches to suit our bowlers. I'm a bowler, so I am unlikely to see anything wrong with it. I understand the complaints and I do appreciate there are wider areas to consider than the winning of a championship game, but the other side of the coin is that we, as players, are under pressure from our committee and our members. Salaries have gone up at county level and so there is more responsibility for us to do well. There are always those who demand to know why I can take a hat-trick for England but can't do it for Derbyshire, so if we play our home games on pitches that give me a better chance, I am not going to complain.

Pragmatic, predictable and blameless. It is not Cork's fault that Derbyshire have played on some dubious pitches, it is the fault of those who run the club and of the system in which the county game continues to operate, a system that is crying out for reforms that would finally overthrow the petty jealousies of members and committees and do what is right for the future of the game as a whole. The central employment of groundsmen – paid by the Test and County Cricket Board to produce the best possible surfaces at all grounds and at all times – would be a start, for it would reduce the potential for cynical manoeuvring.

But county cricket has more to address than this. Much more. If it took a long look at itself it would see that where some other sports (and I stress the some) have moved towards the twenty-first century by upgrading their facilities to attract spectators and their money, cricket has been slow to follow suit. Catering on county grounds remains generally deplorable; the standard of seating on some is still primitive; and the unwelcoming attitude of the staff employed by others is an active deterrent. Slowly, economic realities permitting, the majority are now awakening to the need for updated facilities – Hampshire are even creating a spanking new ground where, it is to be fervently hoped, none of the above criticisms will apply. For if they do, if the counties persist in looking inwards and ignoring the progress all around them, then Cardus's 'great multitude' will be a laughable memory in a county game that destroyed itself through misguided self-interest.

Above Clean-cut and well scrubbed, the cricketer of the 1950s dressed for tradition, not for commercialism. Raymond Illingworth is pictured batting for Yorkshire against MCC at Lord's in 1957, at the age of twenty-four. *(S&G)*

Left When Kerry Packer made his swoop in the late 1970s, cricketers could suddenly make serious money from the game. Graham Gooch, recalled to the England side, waits to bat against India. *(P. Eagar)*

Cricket for the twenty-first century. The players wear garish pyjamas and the grass is scarred by sponsors' logos. Dominic Cork, a modern cricketer and proud of it, appeals successfully for lbw against Gary Kirsten of South Africa. *(G. Morris)*

Bob Taylor represented the best of tradition, diplomacy and undemonstrative skill. He may not have enjoyed the excesses of today. *(P. Eagar)*

The Essex side of the 1970s and 1980s managed to entertain while winning trophies. Keith Pont, *right*, seen being helped into the team bus, and Ray East, *below*, taking an unscheduled drinks break, were two of their clown princes. *(Courtesy of Essex CCC)*

Right Physical training was not a factor in Illingworth's playing days, nor even in the early years of Gooch's career. Gooch, however, took it upon himself to get fitter by pounding the streets of Essex. *(Courtesy of Essex CCC)* *Below* Meanwhile, the modern West Indies teams had their litheness maximized by the attentions of the Australian-born trainer Dennis Waight. *(P. Eagar)*

The changing faces of one-day cricket: *above*, Geoffrey Boycott on his way to a century in the 1965 Gillette Cup final; and Graeme Hick, *below*, in full-colour regalia, thirty years on. *(S&G/G. Morris)*

The most fundamental change in cricket's audience attraction
has been the introduction of floodlights, pioneered by Kerry
Packer and now part of the seasonal routine in Australia and
South Africa and spreading fast elsewhere. *(G. Morris)*

The 1949 New Zealand touring team arrive at Southhampton in what, then, was the traditional style – by ship. *(S&G)*

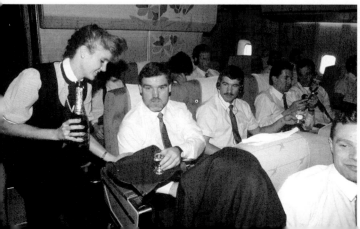

Nowadays, aircraft availability intensifies the schedules of every cricketer. *Above* David Gower's expedition in a Tiger Moth was not part of the tour itinerary...but Mike Gatting's flight, *left*, certainly was. *(G. Morris)*

Thoroughly modern men: Darren Gough *(left)* and Dominic Cork
with the accessories of the 1990s cricketer. *(G. Morris)*

Michael Atherton may be captain of England but he has never seen
why this should mean he must shave every day. *(P. Eagar)*

Above A sign of the times in the early 1970s, when English cricket embraced overseas players too avidly. Five Warwickshire players took part in a Test match at the Oval and four of them were on the West Indies side. *From left to right:* Lance Gibbs, Alvin Kallicharran, Dennis Amiss, Rohan Kanhai and Deryck Murray. *(K. Kelly)*

Mike Brearley in one of the first and most homespun of helmets. *(P. Eagar)*

7

Dress Standards and Discipline

The cricketers of the eighteenth century were nothing if not dapper, judging by the detailed description of their accepted dress standards printed in *Wisden*. They were expected to wear the following listed from top to toe: three-cornered or jockey hats, often with silver or gold lace; shirts, generally frilled; nankeen breeches; silk stockings and buckled shoes. Come 1815, however, the game witnessed the first indication of the falling standards that, so some insist, have been plummeting depressingly ever since. Trousers were introduced to replace breeches and the shirts no longer needed frills, though high collars and bow ties were now de rigueur. The silk stockings had gone too, and black Oxford shoes, without demonstrative buckles, were considered adequate, while the first sign of the influence of professional players was, for some reason, thought to be the wearing of wide braces.

The modern player would have words for this garb and 'smart' would not be among them. And yet, even as the twenty-first century approaches and informality spreads its wings ever wider, the suspicion persists that there is a correlation between dressing well and playing well; or, to take the point further still, that the dress standards of a team and its individuals accurately reflect the general conduct therein.

Conduct is the window of any team's image, and image has never been so precious to the game as it is now.

Forty years ago, in July 1955, E. W. (Jim) Swanton, then the cricket correspondent of the *Daily Telegraph* and now, though an advanced octogenarian, still an esteemed and trenchant contributor to that newspaper, wrote, in essence, a letter to himself. Published on the letters page of his own newspaper, it denounced the 'scruffy' dress of young spectators at that summer's Varsity match and, still more heinous, the fact that certain Cambridge players had omitted to wear their traditional light blue caps on the field. Swanton thundered: 'One was left wondering: does the shoddy dress of many of the undergraduate spectators, the shedding by cricketers of part of their historic uniform, derive from the same basic cause, a weakened sense of personal dignity and good manners? Are the young gentlemen of 1955, outwardly so polite to their seniors, intentionally cocking a snook at the past?'

Although, inevitably, the passing years altered expectations, there was an echo of this indignation two generations later. The England team, captained by Graham Gooch and managed by his mentor from Essex, Keith Fletcher, performed abysmally to lose a Test series in India 3–0. Their cricket was shabby in conception and execution and yet, as a faithful indicator of priorities among the blazered ranks who administrate (and, to some extent, who watch) cricket, the loudest disapproval of that year was directed not towards the standards of play but at standards of dress. At the deflating end of yet another Test defeat in broiling heat, the England players, caked in sweat and dust, shuffled back on to the ground for the presentation ceremonies that, ritually and protractedly, follow every game on the subcontinent. To be kind, they were clad informally. To be harsh, as many were inclined to be, they presented such a shambolic and disunited front that any prospect of being widely perceived as losing with dignity and graciousness had been lost. When the tour manager, the capable and approachable Lancastrian Bob Bennett, was then unwise enough to be photographed conducting a press conference in shorts and T-shirt, it was enough in many eyes to damn the conduct of the tour more comprehensively than the shocking results could ever have done.

We British remain true to our traditions when it comes to this sort of thing. We do stand on ceremony, and we think poorly of any – especially of our own – who decline to do so. This may be construed as stuffy, pompous and obsolete thinking, and when taken to intolerant extremes, perhaps it is. But the essential point is that cricket is a team game and that a team might just perform with more focus and harmony if the players dress similarly and well.

Gooch, although saddled with the stigma of having led the infamous Indian tour, would not disagree with this and, when on public display in the course of his job, habitually dresses immaculately himself. But the interesting thing is that the view is shared, with some passion, by two men as far apart in our generation scale as Raymond Illingworth and Dominic Cork, the one having launched his career even before E. W. Swanton wrote his enraged letter about Varsity standards and the other being no more than a young hopeful when Gooch's tour set off for India.

Illingworth remained a stickler for such standards when he took over as chairman of the England selectors and did not much care for the need to adjust his sights to modernism. He traces his opinions back to his earliest cricketing days. 'It was bred into you at Yorkshire,' he explains with a certain pride, 'and they are still the smartest side in the country today. Our rules were that you turned up well shaven each morning and wore a jacket and tie every match day. I would like to see that enforced again now around the counties and especially in the England team. You should be proud to play for England, and that should reflect in your dress.'

Cork claims that it does, but then he is in this regard a

defender of old-fashioned but worthy principles. He is also a snappy dresser, and his style is complemented by a head of hair that, for some extraordinary reason, never seems to have a strand out of place even when he is bowling his 25th over of an unforgivingly hot day.

> I agree that a shirt, tie and blazer should be the code, certainly on the first day of each match. The same standards should apply on the field and I certainly make sure I never go out with dirty whites or boots. I think there is a lot of pride in appearance among modern players, right down to the little things like making sure their shoes are polished. At Derbyshire, we have certain rules, the strictest of which is that players must not wear jeans, either at the ground or in the hotel when on away trips. It's fair enough – people recognize you and judge you on such things.

Doubtless, Cork would not suggest that his generation should re-adopt the stiff formality that was maintained without question by international teams of Illingworth's day. There is a photograph in my collection from the 1962–3 England tour to Australia. Tom Graveney, Fred Titmus, Colin Cowdrey, Ken Barrington and Illingworth himself are pictured outside their Melbourne hotel before heading off for a round of golf. All of them are dressed in blazer and tie. Compare this with the England teams of thirty-odd years later, basically free to dress as they please on such days off and also permitted to wear their choice from a bewildering range of complimentary-issue sports shirts when travelling, so that it is possible to discern they were a team only by recognizing their faces. Other national teams have similarly relaxed their dress codes, although, interestingly, considering that stuffiness is by no means one of their national characteristics, the West Indies' rules remain stricter than most. When two of their players,

Curtly Ambrose and Kenny Benjamin, chose to ignore the strictures about travelling-day dress on the England tour of 1995, both were fined.

Not all contemporary players consider outward appearance to be important. Indeed, meticulously professional though he is in other respects, Michael Atherton's attitude to personal smartness was responsible for a degree of friction with Illingworth when they came to run the affairs of the England team together. Atherton, by nature, is an untidy person, accustomed to the informality of a bachelor flat where he is accountable to nobody but himself for the mess of laundry on the floor. He has never been keen to shave every morning, either, and it was this lapse or fashion statement, depending on your point of view, which brought a frown to the face and an admonishment to the lips of Illingworth.

Indeed, stubble, specifically as worn by England cricketers, became a subject for public debate in the bizarre aftermath of the 1992–3 Indian tour. Ted Dexter, then the chairman of England's selectors and committee, was required to give a report on the tour to a full meeting of the Test and County Cricket Board and it was within this arena that he discovered the level of indignation over the appearance of the players. It was revealed, at a subsequent press conference, that more time had been taken up debating dress standards than playing failings and Dexter, plainly against his better judgement, was pressed to give a comment on the shaving issue. Though he said nothing untoward, his remarks about 'facial hair' were held up to ridicule by that section of the media – and that section of county administrators – who were by then intent on causing his downfall.

Ironically, Illingworth, who succeeded Dexter, did not shy away from the matter of facial hair. Atherton's habit of turning up, especially on practice days, with a growth of stubble was rapidly discouraged. Atherton complied reluctantly: 'It is not something I see as being particularly important,' he said. But,

Illingworth being the boss, he obligingly fished out his razor on a more regular basis.

The point here is not whether Atherton and other unwilling shavers look better or worse with a day's growth on their chin, it is that some will choose to interpret it as a sign of rebellious idleness. Atherton would scoff at this and retort, with justification, that he should be judged by his cricket and his conduct, not by his face. But there are those who think differently, those who make assessments from other standpoints, those who believe that a team's unity of purpose can indeed be judged by the players' turn-out. Most contentious of all is the theory that a team's smartness reflects directly upon their cricket. This can never be proved, but it will for ever be a subject of argument.

Those who propound such theories are, in the main, those who watch their cricket from a traditionalist platform. There is nothing wrong with that, of course, but the distinction is significant. On major match days now, the spectators can be divided into two contrasting groups: those who routinely put on a suit or blazer and wear a tie out of habit, and those who are more likely to come clad in T-shirt and shorts, of which at least the former may be removed in the heat of the day and the full flush of ten cold cans from the ubiquitous Eskie. Vocal contributions are equally diverse. The suits restrict themselves to clapping at appropriate moments; the T-shirts and bare chests are as likely to break into song or chant.

The mentality of the latter group, that of the football terraces transplanted to summer sport, can be wholesome and harmless. It can, in the right environment and with the application of humour and restraint, create a memorable atmosphere. The self-styled 'Barmy Army', consisting mainly of professional people who became backpacking England supporters on tours in the late 1990s, made a lot of noise and drank a lot of beer wherever they went but, apart from some gratuitously offensive chanting, their behaviour was high-spirited rather than reprehensible. Only the 'impostors', as they called them, the trouble-seekers who attached themselves to the group, brought the risk of violence, but this will always be a danger of such demonstrative conduct.

Even if they are essentially peaceable, the Barmies and their type are not welcomed by everyone, for the racket and antics of crowd sections which appear to have lost interest in watching the cricket can be boorish. They can also be maddeningly distracting, not only to other spectators but occasionally to players. The tiresome Mexican Wave, for instance, so inappropriate to a game demanding peaks of concentration every few seconds, should long ago have been outlawed. Instead, at Kingsmead in South Africa during the 1995–6 Test series against England, the smug, animated scoreboard actively encouraged the crowd to perform it.

Anti-social behaviour among the crowd, defended by those who indulge in it as innocent fun for which they have paid their admission money, can be a recipe for anarchy, just as it was on the football terraces of England a generation ago. The shocking lawlessness of those days, the rituals of gang warfare that were relevant to football only inasmuch as the game provided a suitably confrontational stage, have to some extent been diminished by all-seater stadiums, greater vigilance by clubs and the police and, perhaps, an awareness among the law-abiding majority that their game must not fall into the grip of the destructive few. But enough people of that evil persuasion remain actively at liberty for other games to be threatened, and cricket is undoubtedly among them.

English cricket has never yet suffered the crowd disorders that have been known to halt Test matches and one-day internationals on the Indian subcontinent and in the Caribbean. In general, these have resulted from misplaced partisanship overspilling into the unruly throwing of stones, bottles and firecrackers, which has endangered players and, more than once, caused structural damage to grounds. In the latest such instance, in November 1995, nine people were killed when a stand collapsed at the Indian Test ground at Nagpur. Remarkably, the one-day international in progress at the time was completed after the bodies of the dead and injured had been removed.

Elsewhere, crowd trouble has been of a less dramatic, though no less regrettable type. In Australia, and occasionally South Africa, the late-afternoon, alcohol-induced fist-fighting on the grassy banks known as hills was for years expected, contained and regarded by many almost as a savoury part of the day's entertainment, a violent ritual accepted within a spectator sport rather like the fights in an ice-hockey game. Nowadays, it has come under the control of the ground planners who have, largely, built over the grass, and of the security services which have been reinforced around the world. But such behaviour has its legacy now in England, where certain grounds – Headingley notable among them – are suffering from the influx of an element previously known only to football. They arrive dressed for that game, too, wearing the mass-produced soccer tops now sold at great profit by Premiership clubs, and some of them come, it seems, for no other purpose than to get drunk and become competitively abusive. Sometimes, not yet often but worryingly on the increase, this develops into brawling. One domestic limited-overs tie on the Headingley ground in 1995 contained the worst examples of crowd behaviour I had ever seen on an English ground.

Bob Taylor blames the revolutionary days of Kerry Packer and world series cricket for irrevocably altering the behavioural patterns of crowds and players. 'Its supporters didn't want the charm of cricket, the slow bowler spinning the web to a good batsman on a perfect pitch: they wanted heads split open, helmets and bouncers.'

The players will say there is little they can do about unruly crowd behaviour, that it is the province of the ground authorities and the police to weed out the culprits and prevent its spread. They have a point, too. But they must, surely, be aware that their standards, of behaviour and even of appearance, can be a catalyst for crowd disorder in the very same way that the behaviour of footballers still affects their supporters. Sportsmen must always, always, be above any violent reaction to the abuses that will occasionally come their way. The shocking sight of Eric Cantona, Manchester United's volcanic Frenchman, vaulting advertising hoardings at Selhurst Park to aim a kung-fu-style kick at a spectator early in 1995 had its outcome in a court of law, as well as in debates around the country questioning whether Cantona had forfeited his right ever to play professionally again. The same discussions and criminal charges might have resulted when, in 1980, Sylvester Clarke, the giant West Indian fast bowler, took such offence at being pelted by oranges while fielding on the boundary in Multan, Pakistan, that he threw a brick into the crowd, hitting a spectator. The consequences had the victim been killed would have been calamitous for Clarke and the game itself. As it was, he was seriously hurt. Whether they like it or not, professional sportsmen are on a public pedestal where they are liable to be provoked, sometimes to the limit of endurance, by those jealous souls who wish to bring them down. Equally, they will frequently be aped by those who observe them – and this goes as much for what they wear and how they are turned out as it does for their general conduct.

The accepted accessories of the modern cricketer would have seemed outlandish even a generation ago. He does not wear breeches or silk stockings but he does wear gaudy sunglasses, suncream spread thickly across the face like warpaint, and sometimes even a wristwatch. All are invariably supplied free by opportunist commercial outlets. With the possible exception of a captain playing on a ground without a clock, it is a hard to justify the need for anyone to play in a wristwatch: it is a blatant if harmless case of the cricketer as model. It is difficult, however, to argue coherently against sunglasses,

there being both medical and cricketing grounds for support-
ing their use. The pity of it is that they add to the increasing
anonymity of the player, already shrouded behind more layers
of protection, warranted though they doubtless are, than his
predecessors would ever have contemplated. At one stage of
a recent Test match, England's Darren Gough took to bowling
fast while still wearing his bright blue sunshades. For good
measure, he also wore a matching wristwatch. Traditionalists
fumed at the absurdity of it.

Dominic Cork pleads the case for modernity and justifies
his own use of both sunglasses and copious quantities of zinc
cream. 'People must understand the safety element here. I
don't want to have skin cancer or cataracts when I am forty.
You have to take out as many risks as you can in this game,
but I also dispute that it does any harm to cricket's image. I
think it makes the game look better, more glamorous.'

The players' responsibilities to the image of the game are
many and various. One, frequently neglected, is the signing
of autographs. Successive generations have probably all been
at fault here: some players cannot be bothered, some are posi-
tively aggressive in their discouragement; a few will organize
an orderly queue and stand and sign for twenty minutes or
half an hour during an interval or at the end of a day's play.
Jonty Rhodes, very much a cult figure in post-isolation South
African cricket, is as good an example of the patiently compliant as any I have known. Examples of those who consider
the whole thing an imposition and treat approaching
autograph-hunters with anything from condescension to
ignorant scorn, are plentiful, but should perhaps remain
nameless.

Sportsmen are seldom aware of quite how much a moment
of their time can mean, particularly to the idolizing youngster.
As a boy of eleven, attending my first county match at Hove,
I vividly remember training my eyes on the players' seating
area outside the dressing rooms during a break for bad light.

And suddenly, there he was – John Snow, newly graduated to the England side, an athletically rhythmical fast bowler and, most importantly, my hero. He sat down on one of the park-style benches that are an abiding feature of the Sussex ground and began chatting to a girl who evidently admired him for something other than his bowling. At the foot of the pavilion steps, sweaty hands gripping my pen and autograph book, already held open at a selected clean page, I stood first on one foot, then the other, before darting past the ancient gateman and up the steps to hover at the feet of my hero. I have no memory of saying a single word, though I hope I managed to blurt out something polite as I thrust my book towards him. Thankfully, he signed it with a flourish. Remarkably, I can now, thirty years later, count John Snow as a friend. But he would have no memory of the incident, much less any conception of the spring-heeled joy he imparted to a tongue-tied eleven-year-old.

There are occasions, of course, when a player is genuinely embarrassed by the attention. John Lever became extremely well known and more outgoing later in his career but he still shudders when he recalls himself as a shy and unworldly youngster making his county debut on his home-town ground, Ilford, in 1967. 'I will never forget a little boy of about six coming up to me at the end of the first day and asking for my autograph. I didn't know where to put myself and hurriedly signed his scrap of paper before disappearing into the pavilion red-faced with embarrassment.' Lever came to realize the importance of dealing with the cricketing public and did it manfully, even if, like every one of his colleagues, he occasionally grew weary and impatient with the relentless requirement to be polite to bores, the function of whose small talk is primarily that they may boast to their friends of a conversation with the famous.

Bob Taylor is the best cricketer I have ever known at dealing with such types – dealing, too, with the social niceties required at official functions and diplomatic parties on tour in the 1970s and 1980s. A delightful man of permanent, genuine smile, he seemed so utterly at ease in the company from which many players would shy away that one could only conclude that he enjoyed it. It is for this reason that he was admiringly nicknamed Chat by his peers and, very often, left to wave the banner of sociability while others kept their own counsel in a corner of the room.

The modern player is instinctively suspicious of official functions, either at local level or on tour. Veterans such as Taylor will consider this a shame, not only because they used to enjoy them in the days when High Commission parties presented a rare chance to escape from the inhibitions of a tour, but because they recognized them as part of their responsibility to cricket. Yet it has to be recognized that the altered pace of the game has had its effect and that international cricketers, in particular, no longer have times when the pressure is light. Nowadays, at the rarefied level, the strains of performing to the required standard are so much more intense within the tighter schedules that a player can surely be forgiven if he does not seek to be paraded for social viewing too often. He is, after all, under incessant inspection when performing his day job, in which the scrutiny of officialdom and the many branches of the media has never been so searching.

It is too soon to say whether the introduction of match referees for international cricket has had a sobering effect upon on-field conduct. It is not even certain that the innovation was entirely necessary and such misgivings are amplified by events such as those at the Oval in 1994, when Michael Atherton and Fanie de Villiers were both fined by the Australian referee, Peter Burge, for gestures of dissent so minor that they could barely be discerned from the boundary and could not, by any stretch of the imagination, be thought to have brought the game into disrepute. The fact that Atherton's fine followed closely on the heels of the dirt-in-pocket saga and renewed fatuous calls for him to be replaced as England captain only underlined the futility of such gratuitous punishment.

There is a suspicion that the jobs-for-the-boys syndrome exists in this environment and that certain referees will impose themselves, usually with a reprimand for something trivial, simply to justify their presence. But there have been other instances when blatant and serious transgressions of the game's spirit have been punished with staggering leniency or misguided efforts at even-handedness. The shocking events at Old Trafford in 1992, when Javed Miandad and some of his Pakistan players rounded on umpire Roy Palmer with as nasty and aggressive a case of abuse as I have seen, provide one striking example. Graham Gooch was the England captain on that occasion – an innocent, utterly uninvolved England captain – and he was rightly angered when he and his own side were mentioned reprovingly in the subsequent public statement issued by the referee, Conrad Hunte. As Gooch said, 'We had done nothing, not even been involved in the incident, and if any of our players had behaved as some of the Pakistanis did that evening, they would never have represented England again.'

Gooch does not believe, however, that in general on-field behaviour has declined during his long career.

> What has altered more is the solemnity of it all. There were more characters around when I started, because winning was not quite so all-important. It is all a very serious business now and it tends to discourage people from being funny in the middle because someone is always going to misinterpret it. There are instances of sharp practice, but then there always have been, probably since the game was invented. Some people like to make a lot out of ball-tampering but those who make a fuss generally don't know what they are talking about. Picking the

seam, shining the surface with Vaseline — all these things were around when I started. There is nothing new there, and, of course, it still goes on now. All the teams know what to do and I don't think players worry about it overmuch. Certainly, they don't consider it an evil that must be stamped out.

Umpires always say that behaviour is deteriorating but I can't see it. I don't think there is any more nastiness than when I began and, even at Test level, the conduct of the England team has been good for some years.

This last comment was made advisedly. The England team's deportment has, indeed, been irreproachable of late, though only since the end of the 1980s, when Gooch himself took over as captain. In the years immediately prior to this, notably under the leadership of Mike Gatting, England's conduct was sometimes inclined to be surly and confrontational; worse, it was condoned by both Gatting and the then team manager, Micky Stewart, and defended against all criticism with wide-eyed innocence. In Gatting's case, this took the form of high-pitched indignation that anyone should think ill of his players; in Stewart's, a regular disclaimer that he had not seen Broad fail to walk or smash down his stumps or Dilley loudly swear and so on, because he had been in the nets. True or not, it was unhelpful and gave the sad impression of a team whose moral responsibilities had been collectively abandoned.

Perhaps this had been coming for some time. Tony Greig captained England in the mid-1970s, before being seduced by the power and money offered by Kerry Packer, and for all his obvious dynamism and charm, he is blamed — by Bob Taylor for one — for scorning the spirit of the game. 'Greig bears a fair amount of responsibility for the decline in sportsmanship in the English game,' wrote Taylor in his autobiography. 'He was the first England player I remember actively indulging in gamesmanship.' Taylor recalls with disfavour Greig's habits of pointing a dismissed batsman to the pavilion and of 'standing at silly point mouthing at batsmen', and relates that, as Derbyshire captain, he once reported Greig for ungentlemanly conduct when he considered that he had deliberately barged into Eddie Barlow – ironically, another forthright South African – in a Sunday League game.

It is only a short step that carries off-field indiscipline into a match arena and there is no disputing that some of the England sides of the 1980s enjoyed themselves extravagantly outside playing hours, even to the extent where their behaviour could be considered arrogant, above the accepted standards of their lifestyle. This was the era of Ian Botham, in his pomp, and of David Gower, Bob Willis and Allan Lamb. Not for many years had England possessed so many players of such charisma and, as all were gregarious men, it became headline news if one or other of them was thought to have had a drink too many, stayed out too late or behaved offensively in a hotel. It came to a head on the 1983–4 tour of New Zealand, led by Willis, on which lurid newspaper accounts accused the England side of drug-taking in their own dressing room. Nothing was ever substantiated and a subsequent police inquiry was dropped but, some months later, Botham made one of the few confessions of his career when he admitted that he had smoked cannabis. This might have fed the 'no-smoke-without-fire' theories surrounding the New Zealand allegations; undoubtedly, it transmitted a message about Botham that would have startled those who had never given house room to the tales of wild and weird behaviour that he habitually denied. It posed a question-mark against the most famous cricketer of his generation, which, in turn, raised public awareness that cricketers, traditionally held to be gentlemen of unimpeachable background, might not all fit the bill.

And why should they? Why should cricketers be any more saintlike than other sportsmen – indeed, than workers in any other field? The answer is, of course, that they are not, and never have been, either in action or at leisure. There have always been players who behave loutishly on the field, just as there have always been those who drink too much, dress scruffily and generally tarnish the preferred image of the game. But perhaps it has never seemed as important as it does now, that cricket is no longer simply a sport but a competitor for vast sums of money in an entertainment industry with immeasurable television and advertising potential. This may be thought regrettable by many who preferred things as they were, but it cannot be ignored if the game is to progress in good health. Hence the magnified attention on the standards displayed by the players. Hence their ever-increasing level of responsibility.

Occasionally, the acceptable bounds of gamesmanship or sharp practice are breached. One such instance was a televised provincial match in Johannesburg, South Africa, in 1982, in which two batsmen, one from each side, were run out when transparently not attempting a run. The first dismissal was malevolent, the second vengeful, and the sequence inevitably caused great media debate and public outcry. The former captain of South Africa, Alan Melville, delivered his own judgement on the cause of such conduct. 'I'm sure they would not have done it had there been no money at stake. But then, we must realize that the whole spirit of the game today has altered because of money, and sportsmanship and chivalry have disappeared.' It was a damning indictment of the changed times; a warning, echoed by Graham Gooch's comments on solemnity, that the modern game must not take itself too seriously.

Raymond Illingworth cites one area in which he believes moral standards have dropped. 'There is a lot more appealing and shouting now. In the 1950s, ninety-eight per cent of batsmen walked when they knew they were out. Hardly any-one does now, which in turn encourages the fielding side to shout for everything on the basis that while a batsman might get away with one or two borderline decisions by standing his ground, they might in return pick up a wicket they don't really deserve.'

Dominic Cork concedes that this is a part of the modern game but does not accept Illingworth's righteous version of his own playing days. Perhaps he read his England manager's first book, *Spinner's Wicket*, written in 1969, in which he reflects without rancour on the gamesmanship of senior players in the Yorkshire side of that decade. According to Illingworth, Jimmy Binks, the wicketkeeper, was 'always nattering' to opposing batsman, mischievously pointing out 'that ugly so-and-so' Brian Close, who would be creeping within a yard of the bat at short leg or silly point. So maybe nothing really has changed, as Cork maintains:

> People say there is still a lot too much talking on the field and they say it didn't happen in the old days. I don't believe that. Up to a couple of years ago, I personally had too much to say on the pitch, but I have that under control now. I think it's only human nature to show some emotions, though; that it is a perfectly acceptable part of the game and its image, if kept within bounds. There are times in cricket when players will explode, because it is a very frustrating sport. It can knock you down in a single session. I see nothing wrong in expressing your feelings.

Cork is one of those who have emerged from the brat-pack mentality where others of his generation are still marooned. He has learned, with increasing maturity, to tailor his conduct to the requirements of sport in the twenty-first century: dress in smart, modern style to attract attention, but never cause offence; wear the gaudy accessories of the age, warpaint and all; appeal theatrically and often, but always accept the umpire's verdict. These are thoroughly modern standards that might not have done in the days of nankeen breeches and frilled shirts — and would assuredly not have done in Illingworth's Yorkshire side — but then, these are times in which every sport, if it is to prosper, must have its visual colour and excesses, and then learn to control them.

8

They Came From Overseas

It was in 1965 that English cricket began to stretch out a tentative hand of welcome to players from overseas. It was precisely thirty years later that the welcome became so tepid that influential voices proposed it should be withdrawn altogether. Within those three decades, foreign stars had come in large numbers, making an increasingly fine living and, so the anti-foreigner lobby proclaimed, learning their trade for the benefit of their own countries at English expense. The counter-argument was that overseas players raised standards by inspiring the English players around them, and injected glamour into an otherwise insular structure. The supporters of the system, however, decreased as concern over the performances of the England Test team, and resentment about the amount of money counties were settling upon their imports, began to gain the day.

Many people wanted English cricket reclaimed for Englishmen. Some, more mischievously and less sustainably, wanted the England team returned to England as well. Partly as a result of the cosmopolitan nature of Britain's population from the 1960s onwards, and occasionally because opportunist foreigners chose England as their flag of convenience for a cricketing career, the Test team was no longer exclusively the province of those born in the country. Immigrants from the

Caribbean and Australasia accounted for one influx; cricketing refugees from an isolated South Africa for another. The trend has not been unanimously approved of, even among contemporary players.

Robin Smith, Allan Lamb, Graeme Hick, Devon Malcolm and others became successful and popular members of the England team and, despite the legal action of 1995 (and subsequent damages paid to Malcolm and Phillip DeFreitas) that resulted from one scurrilous article in a monthly magazine, none could seriously doubt their wholeheartedness. There were, however, those who believed that national identity, the communal sense of possession and purpose that is such a passionate feature of modern Australian sides, had been eroded from the English game because it was not, any longer, fundamentally English. At least two recent England captains harbour this opinion and would dearly love to be able to address the issue, but know in their hearts that it is already too late.

The opening of the floodgates in the late 1960s, when some counties flagrantly breached the spirit if not the letter of the new legislation by registering more and more players from abroad, and the relaxation of the rules governing residential qualification for England, were responsible for an altered cricketing culture, one that embraced all comers. This was in some ways an admirably liberal philosophy, of course, but after a number of years of wallowing in the attendant glamour, even exoticism, that talented, foreign-born players initially brought to what had been a tired and impecunious English game, the novelty value wore thin. Come the 1990s, and a serious trough for the England side at Test level, there was a growing awareness that the game had lost its focus. Counties were competing to pay huge sums of money to contract overseas players, only some of whom were remotely in the superstar bracket in terms of ability, and increasingly were discovering that many such players were unwilling to do much to justify their salaries. And at international level, England were guilty of what might kindly be thought of as false modesty: the assumption that a player who had come from overseas and qualified to be considered English must, by definition, be better than his English-born peers. It was a blind and slippery road to choose and it led to some bizarre and divisive England selections which, by their apparently positive discrimination towards the newly qualified, caused intense resentment among those who considered themselves at least their equals.

There was, from some sources, a racist element to all this which should not be denied or ignored. From an unpleasant minority, this concentrated on colour. My mailbag at *The Times* has sometimes included monstrous letters on this subject. One, late in 1995, began by asking if I had noticed that England played better when the entire team was white. It continued: 'I know all my friends feel more comfortable with a white team ... Leave out the blacks and play white players. The blacks could play better for their own countries.' The letter was not dignified by a reply.

But if jingoism-turned-racism was an ugly sideshow of the issue, there were serious cricketing reasons for regretting the legacy of the lenient years, and at the winter meeting of the Test and County Cricket Board in December 1995, the board's cricket committee proposed that a complete ban on overseas players should follow the previously agreed moratorium in 1999. The counties, who are the constituents of the TCCB, agreed only to discuss the matter again at their spring meeting. Most, mindful primarily of the perceived box-office draw (rarely fulfilled in practice) of the big foreign names, were deeply unhappy about the proposal, though their opposition was based on some dubious premises and once again studiously overlooked the greater good of the English game that was the principal motivator of the proposal.

Overseas players are nothing new. Late in the nineteenth century, Australians such as Billy Midwinter plied their trade in the county game. It was a contentious practice then, too, and it faded into disuse due to legislation restricting counties wishing to use foreigners to players who had lived continuously within their boundaries for two years. During the 1950s, there was a group of Australians in county cricket who met these requirements, including Colin McCool and Bill Alley at Somerset and Bruce Dooland at Trent Bridge, but they were players who had abandoned Test ambitions in their native land and had come to live permanently in England.

The first relaxation of the rules came in 1963, when overseas players were allowed to play abroad in the English winter. In the ensuing five seasons, fifty-seven cricketers born outside the United Kingdom played in the County Championship, Kent and Warwickshire employing five each. But this was never going to be the end of the adjustments and when, in 1965, a proposal by Nottinghamshire to allow one instant overseas registration was rejected, it merely delayed the inevitable. The county game was in a deep rut, negative cricket and declining crowds were putting some clubs at risk of imminent bankruptcy, and the appeal of injecting interest through names that were, in that era, more famous than their faces and styles was naturally immense. The *Cricketer* magazine mounted a campaign in support of instant registrations and, in 1966, the Clark Report – produced by a working party of distinguished current and former players – included a recommendation to that effect. As the vast majority of the reforms they mooted for the game were sound and prophetic but, in the main, rejected, it was ironic that this one found favour.

There was now an irresistible momentum towards the change and when it was adopted, in 1967, enabling counties to contract an overseas player once every three years, it was widely acclaimed. *Wisden* declared it to be the 'biggest step forward in recent years' and E. W. Swanton, writing in the *Daily Telegraph*, pronounced: 'However things turn out, I believe that, in the long run, even the counties who oppose the change may live to bless it.' And, for a tolerably long run, so they did.

England possesses the only full-time professional cricket circuit in the world. Due to its geographical position it also happens to be the only Test-playing country whose season spans the northern hemisphere summer. So the attractions were mutual: foreign players, otherwise forced to seek temporary work with an understanding employer out of season, could now occupy themselves playing cricket all year round, and, through the money the counties were prepared to pay, significantly increase their standard of living at the same time.

The first draft of instant registrations was a fascinating mix. There were four West Indians – Gary Sobers, Rohan Kanhai, Vanburn Holder and Geoffrey Greenidge; four South Africans – Mike Procter, Barry Richards, Lee Irvine and Hylton Ackerman; two Pakistanis – Asif Iqbal and Majid Khan; and one each from India (Farokh Engineer) and Australia (Greg Chappell). They fell into two different categories, too, for while some counties were prepared to break the bank for the best, Sobers for instance, others gambled on young and relatively unproven talent. Richards and Procter were both twenty-two and had yet to play Test cricket; Greg Chappell was only nineteen. The distinction between the registering of Chappell and Sobers, for instance, is an important one in the context of the trends that have followed.

Chappell joined Somerset for only £1,000 a year, which placed him on a par with the majority of the English-born players of the time. His initiation was rigorous – in his first match against Yorkshire he went into bat on a hat-trick – but in the course of his two years at the club he avers that he learned an immense amount, both as a man and as a cricketer. It was an early instance of the overseas-player system acting as an offshore finishing school, nursing future opponents towards maturity and fulfilment, educating them in many things that they could subsequently use against England at international level.

Sobers was a different case entirely, for there was little left for him to learn but plenty for him to impart to those around him. He had been a sensation on the West Indies tour of England in 1966, scoring 722 runs in the series, taking 20 wickets and holding some stunning catches close to the wicket, quite apart from charming all who saw him with his languid athleticism and easy manner. He was approached by seven counties following the formal end of restricted entry, and his acceptance of a £7,000 offer from Nottinghamshire made him the highest-paid cricketer in the world. Sobers did not let them down: in his first season, 1968, he scored almost 1,600 first-class runs and took 83 wickets. By way of mind-boggling bonus, he also hit six sixes in an over off Glamorgan's subsequently long-suffering Malcolm Nash, a feat that by happy coincidence was captured by television cameras at Swansea and has since been replayed as many times as any sporting clip in the vaults of Broadcasting House. Notts rose from sixteenth to fourth place in the County Championship and could feel mightily pleased with their investment on all but one front: even Sobers, unrivalled as the greatest all-round cricketer in the world, had no great effect on their attendances at Trent Bridge. This ought to have served as a warning – and certainly it was to prove an accurate gauge – but by now the counties had been seduced to a point where the overseas player was considered the answer to everything.

While the clubs now voted themselves ever-increasing rights to sign up foreigners, home-grown players were not quite so ecstatic about the trend. In 1969, Raymond Illingworth wrote: 'For years, counties have been saying that they cannot pay their own players £1,000. Yet all of a sudden they can find £4,000 or £5,000 for a star from the West Indies, Australia or South Africa. Of course, some of these players are better than the English county players, but not four or five times better.' Yorkshire, of course, were alone in resisting the free-for-all and stood true to their principles for twenty-five years. But this was not the sole reason for Illingworth's resent-

ment. Apart from the financial discrepancies, which an England player like himself would understandably condemn as
unfair, he felt from an early stage that the drawbacks of the
scheme would outweigh its advantages. On balance, and with
the inestimable benefit of hindsight, I believe he is correct.

When Warwickshire won the 1972 County Championship,
they were helped by no fewer than four West Indians – Rohan
Kanhai, Alvin Kallicharran, Lance Gibbs and Deryck Murray.
What incentive did that give to the young, aspiring English
players on their staff, obliged to compete for one of seven
available places rather than one of eleven? A year later, the title
was won by Hampshire, whose team included Barry Richards
(South Africa), Gordon Greenidge (West Indies) and David
O'Sullivan (New Zealand). Nobody could doubt the pedigree
of Richards and Greenidge, who became the most feared and
respected opening pair in county cricket, but did O'Sullivan,
a left-arm spin bowler of modest accomplishments, really rate
a place ahead of a young English slow bowler? Apparently
not, because the following year he was released, only for
Hampshire to add a second West Indian to their string in the
fast bowler Andy Roberts.

Not every county ate so greedily at the trough. Some con-
tented themselves with one overseas player at a time and chose
skilfully within their self-imposed limitation. Essex were perhaps the best example of such frugality, although, at least at
first, their policy was dictated by the fact that they had very
little money to spend. Their first import was Lee Irvine, the
hard-hitting South African left-hander who, like Richards and
Procter, was to suffer the cruelly rapid termination of his Test
career. Irvine, now a businessman and television commentator
living in Johannesburg, spent two seasons with Essex at the
time when they still played nomadically, staging festival weeks
at six or seven grounds around the county. He recalls playing
at grounds with only one unreliable shower, and travelling
back to his rented home by train, unwashed and still in his

cricket kit. He remembers the splinters and protruding nails on the wooden floor of the old shack-like pavilion at Chelmsford, which was responsible for instilling into a generation of Essex cricketers the habit of putting their socks and shoes on first when dressing at the end of a day's play. And, despite such deprivations, despite the fact that he was hardly paid a princely sum, he says he wished he had stayed longer. 'I learned so much about the game in those two years,' he reflects, 'mainly from listening to Gordon Barker and from watching Keith Fletcher. They were my mentors and, for me, county cricket was an enjoyable education.'

Essex subsequently used Keith Boyce, Kenny McEwan and Norbert Phillip, each of whom, in their different ways, fitted snugly into the singular, somewhat manic atmosphere of their dressing room. But even Essex had their flops, such as a South African called Hugh Page, signed as a potentially destructive fast bowler, who proved such a disappointment that, long before the end of his season, he was considered unworthy of a place in the side. Here was proof that even the best-run clubs could fall foul of the compulsion to take advantage of the permitted quota of foreigners. Nobody had really known what Page was capable of, but Essex signed him anyway, because they had a vacancy and because he was available. Certain other counties, Surrey and Glamorgan prominent among them, have committed similar follies more than once.

During the 1970s, overseas players – that is, men who were not qualified to play at Test level for England – made up 15 per cent of the cricketing workforce. Too much; far too much. Slight reductions were imposed in 1979, after which year no county was permitted to play more than two imports in any game, but this did not stop Sussex, for instance, registering Imran Khan, Garth le Roux and Kepler Wessels and rotating the man with a match off according to fitness and conditions. Not only was it a mighty strain on the club finances to support three prominent international cricketers and all their various demands, it was also an active disincentive to the aspiring young Englishman. Gradually, an awareness of this situation began to dawn. John Woodcock, writing the editor's notes in the 1981 *Wisden*, declared: 'The extent to which these cricketers from abroad are being allowed to hinder the progress of young English talent has become an intolerable frustration to the England selectors.' Alec Bedser and Peter May, successive chairmen of selectors, had consistently pleaded for a reduction in the numbers of imports, but both were thwarted by the English system, in which decisions of any significance are taken by the counties. Asking them to do away with the foreign stars they coveted, and fondly imagined to be the source of future glories, was like the proverbial hopeless cause of asking turkeys to vote for Christmas.

The overseas players themselves could hardly be expected to make a case for their expulsion, either. Imran Khan and Richard Hadlee were among those who gave spirited and articulate defences of the system, pointing out quite validly that all young players should be able to learn and improve from close acquaintance with other cricketers of their stature. An alternative view, however, came from Martin Crowe, an enigmatic character and indirectly the cause of the strife which saw Ian Botham depart bitterly from Somerset in the wake of their preference of Crowe as overseas player to either Vivian Richards or Joel Garner. Whether that decision was correct is not now the issue. Crowe had spent a summer stimulating the ambitions and attitudes of Somerset's second team before graduating to the first-class side, and at the end of his time with the club he doubted whether the system was working. 'In my experience,' he said, 'the home-grown kids have sub-consciously said [of their overseas player], "Oh, he'll do it – he'll take the wickets and score the runs." And it shows.' Crowe's view, then, was that the use of foreign stars did not so much educate English youngsters as soothe them into a dangerous complacency.

The domination of almost two decades of Test cricket by the West Indies is not to be glibly explained away by any single factor, but a pertinent contribution was made by the fact that the great majority of their players had been toughened and polished by serving time on the county circuit. A proportion of them, such as Malcolm Marshall, Vivian Richards and Clive Lloyd, also put a good deal back into their chosen clubs and became deservedly revered figures. But the facile correlation between West Indians and success led counties with a vacancy to the belief that any West Indian was better than any Englishman and this was not only insulting but misguided. Not every signing could bring dividends, of course, but some were very evidently long shots, redolent of desperation.

The public, however, was not routinely taken in. The excitement caused by the first consignments of foreigners in the late 1960s and early 1970s had long since abated and the followers of county clubs were now inclined to be more judgemental. The overseas player no longer had rarity value and nor, in most cases, did he arrive with an excellent reputation not known to an English audience. The supporters rightly felt entitled to judge as they saw, and in some cases they were singularly unimpressed by surly, unapproachable individuals who would try when it suited them and decline to play on the slightest pretext of unfitness. Many overseas players have been held in genuine affection and esteem, but almost as many have not. In general, their benefits – a mark of their relationship with the club's supporters – have been lower than those of English players and their books, whether anecdotal or technical, have sold poorly within an English market keener to read about the thoughts and experiences of their home-grown heroes.

Just occasionally, however, the arrival of an import creates vast interest, as was the case at Edgbaston in 1994. Warwickshire had initially signed the Indian all-rounder Manoj Prabhakar as a one-year replacement for their South African fast bowler Allan Donald, who would be engaged on Test duty that summer. When Prabhakar was ruled out on fitness grounds, the club moved instead for a young West Indian batsman of soaring reputation. Terms were agreed, the contract was signed and a matter of weeks later, Brian Lara scored 375 against England at the St John's Recreation Ground in Antigua, breaking the Test record and sparking a stampede of potential new members to the Edgbaston offices. It was a lucky break for Warwickshire, even more so when Lara followed up his feat by scoring 501 not out against Durham within a month of joining them, but although he did, on a short-term basis, bring people through the gates in substantial numbers, and helped Warwickshire to the very brink of a clean sweep of the four domestic competitions, his stay with the club was not without its problems. Lara adopted a high-handed attitude, often turning up late and taking a number of reluctantly authorized breaks to fly home to Trinidad. He had a well-chronicled spat on the field with his captain, Dermot Reeve, and, though he played many fine innings for the county and justified his salary to all but the harshest observer, he seemed disinclined to earn the respect of his colleagues as a team-mate and a person, rather than simply as a run-scorer. The following year, if given a choice between Lara and Donald, almost all would have opted for the unstinting South African, and it was no great surprise when the club's hasty commitment to a three-year contract for Lara was first reduced and then, amid mutual disenchantment, scrapped altogether.

Donald, who had been slighted by this deal being struck when he was about to return to Warwickshire for the 1995 season, bowled his heart out all summer to help the club retain the County Championship and, simultaneously, considered a variety of future possibilities. He could have joined a rival club for a small fortune, for at least two counties were willing to fork out £90,000 for his signature; in the end he decided to stay at Edgbaston as a bowling coach. Doubtless his decision did not cause him financial suffering, but that is beside the point. The difference between Donald's affinity with Warwickshire and Lara's passing flirtation was lost on few.

There are times when the workaday English professionals are unworthily jealous of the rewards being commanded by others, but occasionally their principle is their guiding light. The case of Andrew Symonds orchestrated a rare strength of feeling in the game that was influenced by neither personal animosity to Symonds nor financial matters. Symonds, for the record, earned the relative pittance of £8,000 playing for Gloucestershire in 1994 and could have commanded five times that figure the following summer. His ability was not in doubt, but his qualification to play county cricket as an Englishman most certainly was. Symonds was born in Birmingham but brought up, as an adopted child, in Queensland, Australia. He considered himself to be Australian and, when scoring a century against the touring England side late in 1994, told the assembled media that he had no intention or desire to play Test cricket for any other country. This alone enraged many players, but when he subsequently rejected an invitation to play for England A in Pakistan, he nailed his colours firmly to the mast. Still Gloucestershire pursued their intention to sign him on a new, long-term contract, and even a toughening-up of the declaration procedure governing such qualification matters did not deter them. Legally, they and Symonds were probably acting within their rights; morally, in the view of the playing workforce, they were countenancing an abuse of the system, a sham. Prominent players, the England captain Michael Atherton among them, spoke seriously of strike action on the issue.

Although this was a slightly separate question from that of overseas players, many of the same objections applied. Atherton was among those who had come round to the view that England should go it alone with home-bred cricketers. Raymond Illingworth, his chairman of selectors at England level, wholeheartedly agreed. A contrary view was put by Dominic Cork, who pointed out how much he personally had learned from the presence at Derbyshire of Michael Holding, John Wright and Mohammed Azharudin. 'I think they should still be involved,' he said. 'If they are the right type, prepared to put something into their clubs, they can add spice and enjoyment to players and spectators alike. They can make the game look so easy, and English players should be able to learn from them.' But Cork added a rider, voicing the suspicions of many, the most obvious of several reasons for believing that the import has had his day: 'There are certain overseas players who demand £100,000, don't want to bother with fielding and turn up just to bat and bowl. They think they have done their job but all they have really done is to take the money and run.'

9

Fads and Fashions

Cricket is a reactionary game, for good as well as selfish reasons, and its native resistance to change has, by and large, protected its outward appearance. Until the late 1970s, indeed, the look of a cricket ground on any given match day had altered little since the Second World War. The players dressed in white, without fashion accessories, and there were only minor periodical changes in the cut of their flannels or shirts; the umpires wore long white coats and imposed their character upon the scene by the veracity, and natural fallibility, of their decision-making; sightscreens and boundary fences were white and usually unadorned by advertisements; scoreboards were comforting wooden structures of black or green with the numbers operated manually on rollers. These were the evocative images of cricket: it was how it had been for generations; how, we thought, it should always remain.

The shift to modernity has been, by cricketing standards, painfully swift. Cricket is no longer a game of traditional symmetries, of greens and whites where they had for so long belonged. It has embraced first the garishness of a commercial age in which to gain attention it is necessary to startle, and now, remorselessly, the machinery of a technological age. These have given cricket new colours, new images and a new audience, but the latter has taken away human frailty and imposed safety in anonymity. The fact that it was inevitable, also financially desirable for all those involved, does not mean its advent is without sadness.

The most profound effect of all this is that the game has lost that reassuring stability, the sense that one could be without it for years at a time yet still know, by shutting one's eyes and conjuring up fond memories, exactly how it still appeared. Nowadays, it is a fickle game, susceptible to fads and fashions, manipulated by the arms of commerce and of the computer freeway rather than by the traditional cricketing values. And this applies to the players, their equipment and accessories, and to umpires, now slaves to their own technology, as much as it does to the peripheries of the game, like white balls and black sightscreens at night, animated electronic scoreboards and public-address announcers who are not so much animated as hysterical. Sometimes, amid the modish modernity of cricket's revolution, it is difficult to recall accurately just how constant, how timeless a game it was, and so relatively recently.

The professional cricketer's uniform, or working clothes, were the first paraphernalia to display the influence of the new age. Once the use of pads (adopted in crude form in 1800 and derided by those who believed in macho values) and gloves (1827) had become common, the contents of the cricketer's kitbag changed little until the 1970s. And even when Raymond Illingworth set out on his long career, it was not a sponsored or subsidized kitbag. 'When I started, I bought all my own gear,' he says. 'The club gave us our sweaters and, when we'd earned them, our caps, but nothing else. I used Senior County bats and I had my flannels made up by a man named Jack Appleyard. They were good ones, too. He charged £5 a pair, which was a lot of money in those days, but they were well made and lasted a long time.'

Such frugality belongs to a world of which the modern player knows little. Dominic Cork would not expect to spend his own money on his kit, any more than he would expect to be out of pocket for his meals and travel during a match, or to provide his own car. Yet all such obligations were accepted without question by the cricketers of Illingworth's day. Cork, indeed, does rather better than simply having his equipment provided free of cost. He is paid to use it, in some cases quite handsomely, as the myriad of sports-gear companies compete to attract business by bragging about which famous players are in their 'stable'. Many cricketers now have a portfolio of such sponsorships, endorsing different companies' bats, boots, gloves and maybe the ubiquitous sunglasses and wristwatches. Whether this actually has any impact on the sales of the product concerned is for the companies and their market-research boffins to decide but, especially during the get-rich-quick 1980s, product endorsement became a gravy train for cricketers – and not just those who, like Cork, could be thought to have earned such a perk through performances at the highest level. Many workaday county players, has-beens and never-will-bes on the broader canvas of fame, were commanding lucrative equipment contracts. This was the daft, irrational era in which the perception that cricket was booming with a new audience led book publishers – traditionally scrupulous and Scrooge-like – to lavish contracts upon anyone who had been mentioned in dispatches at an England selection meeting, and quite a few who had not. Inevitably, their books had a narrow appeal, if any at all, and the gradual dawning among publishing houses of the error of their ways led, along with the onset of recession, to a more strictly selective sanctioning of cricketers bursting into print. To some degree, the same thing happened with the equipment companies, as Graham Gooch confirms.

They are choosier now than they were during the 1980s. They have to be. The recession hit them, like everyone else, and they can't be giving out contracts, cash and free gear to everyone on a club's staff. It just isn't viable and nor, in the long run, is it good for the young players. It's the same syndrome as sponsored cars – if you start giving players too many perks before they have done anything to earn them, they will think they have arrived. It's a recipe for complacency.

Gooch was given bats, gloves and pads – though no cash – by the Surridge company when he signed for Essex in 1973. Two years later, when he made his England debut and became a marketable item, he changed stables and took Gray–Nicholls equipment, naturally enough with a cheque attached, but he was subsequently to return to Surridges, whose bats he still endorses today.

No player of ambition can afford to be casual about his kit but there can have been few cricketers of any generation more meticulous about equipment than Gooch. He gives the credit for this to Keith Fletcher, his mentor in so many ways, but he developed his own, singular habits with his kit, rightly regarding each and every piece as a tool of the trade, designed to help him achieve the best possible results. 'Everything,' recalls his friend and former team-mate John Lever, 'from bat to gloves, pads, helmet – even that familiar floppy sunhat – has to be just right for him. He would often go back to the manufacturers whose products were carrying his name with suggested improvements which would benefit other players at every level.' Just one instance of Gooch's innovations is a Velcro strip he designed as an attachment to the inside of his thigh pad. In hot weather, he would use it to strap a flannel to his leg to soak up the sweat. It is a simple but effective device since copied by many other batsmen.

Equipment is, of course, being developed and improved all the time, which makes it somewhat surprising that so much remains to be done. Take gloves, for instance. One would have thought they were the most basic part of a cricketer's accessories, and yet, despite more than 170 years of development, no one has ever hit upon anything entirely satisfactory. Gooch carries in his bag four pairs of identical batting gloves, carefully initialled and numbered, GAG1 to GAG4. The scrupulous customizing is more unusual than the quantity he uses; indeed, other modern players often go further. Michael Atherton takes ten pairs of gloves on tour with him, being particular about wearing fresh gloves whenever possible, and Robin Smith, a compulsive changer of gloves during a long innings, gets through even more. Everyone has their own fads about gloves and their design, but none of these international batsmen, nor anyone else, for that matter, has managed to find a glove that overcomes, or even substantially reduces the fundamental risk of a batsman having his fingers broken. Outlandish variations have come and gone – remember the vast, mitten-backed model worn by Tony Greig in the 1970s? – but there is no decline in the number of finger injuries. Rather the opposite, in fact, as uneven pitches, combined with the modern preponderance of fast bowling, produce regular epidemics of cracked and fractured digits. In this regard, cricket and technology have failed each other.

With apologies to the more inventive of batmakers, the development of bats owes less to science than to fashion. Leaving aside the infamous aluminium bat, a tacky extension of Dennis Lillee's money-making powers in the 1970s, they are still carved of willow, still essentially the same shape, length and fallible width. Only the weight changes with the tide, and it will surprise many to learn that the most recent trend towards heavy bats is nothing compared to their weight in the early nineteenth century. It is said that William Ward made a then record score of 278 in the 1820 season wielding a bat that weighed 4lb 2oz. He must have had extremely weary arms at the end of it all.

For much of the twentieth century, the preference was for very much lighter bats, often of not much more than half the weight of the one used by the good Mr Ward. Tony Greig, who was nothing if not a cricketing revolutionary, was perhaps the first man in modern times to order a bat of 3lb in weight and he had the size to carry it off. Gooch, who began his Test career with a bat weighing 2lb 8oz, used gradually heavier bats through the 1980s, peaking with a three-pounder. But, late in his career, his preferences altered again towards the lighter blade. 'It is a faddish thing these days,' he confirmed. 'Once a few players begin thinking that we should use heavier or lighter bats, the rest will follow.' There are, however, some interesting distinctions. India's two modern batting princes are Mohammed Azharudin and Sachin Tendulkar. Neither is a big man, but Tendulkar is significantly the smaller. Azharudin uses a 2lb 4oz bat and the tiny Tendulkar prefers one about 8oz heavier.

It is difficult for the 1990s cricketer to conceive of a time when pads, gloves and the abdominal 'box' were the only regulation protection worn by batsmen, and when some even disdained gloves. Nowadays, even tail-end batsmen, who were once expected to do no more than hold up an end in an emergency, and dressed accordingly, appear in the middle clad for battle. The batsman's suit of armour is now virtually head-to-toe, as Dominic Cork describes.

> I began wearing a helmet for batting when I was a teenager in the Minor Counties and it is as much a part of my essential uniform as pads and gloves. I also wear a chest guard, arm guards and a big thigh pad, all of which go on by routine, not only when the pitch is lively or the bowling especially hostile. My gloves are designed especially for me and have plastic-coated shock-absorbers in each finger, just to lessen the risk. I will do everything I can to avoid injury while I am batting. My main job is to bowl, and I can't do that if I've got broken fingers or ribs.'

No matter how much one may regret the visual image such protection now conveys, it is impossible to dispute Cork's logic. Indeed, perhaps the most surprising aspect of it is that it was not used sooner. These extensive safety measures have been second nature only to his generation, having been the subject of much experimentation by the last. Helmets were unknown until the late 1970s, when the curious, homespun versions began to appear. Mike Brearley designed what was little more than an adjunct to the cap, two absorbent white flaps protecting his temples. It looked ridiculous and, cricketers being vain creatures, it was never going to catch on, but it planted an idea that was not to be lightly discarded. At the other end of the subtlety scale, Dennis Amiss, the Warwick-shire and England opening batsman, wore the kind of vast, bulky helmet more readily associated with astronauts, or maybe with Barry Sheene. He, too, was mocked, but the momentum was now unstoppable and within a few years helmets of a more sophisticated and regulated design were being worn habitually by the vast majority of Test and first-class players. Nowadays, the habit has spread downwards through the game, to league matches on a Saturday afternoon, even village and school games, where, though it will be vigor-ously defended as 'a good habit to get into', the use of helmets owes more to the image-consciousness of those trying to imi-tate their heroes than to any genuine safety element.

There are general arguments against helmets even now, usually championed by those who played in a time before they were thought necessary. It can validly be claimed that they encourage lazy habits in batsmen, who may be struck around the head by balls they would otherwise have avoided more alertly. It remains a moot point whether they have any detrimental effect on technique, or whether the visors and grilles decrease a batsman's peripheral vision. It can certainly be said that they are the single greatest advertisement of the fundamental change in the nature of the modern game – more gladiatorial, arguably more glamorous, but certainly less personal.

Umpiring has also lost much of its personal touch. It is not that the characters have disappeared from the job, for demonstrably they have not, but the scrutiny that now accompanies it, and the technology that is a part of it, do not encourage much in the way of relaxed cordiality. In his 1934 book *Good Days*, Neville Cardus wrote: 'The umpire at cricket is like the geyser in the bathroom; we cannot do without it, yet we notice it only when it is out of order.' To some extent, this remains the case, but whereas in Cardus's day the quality of umpiring decisions was simply a matter of debate and conjecture, it is now increasingly a matter of fact, proved and analysed ad nauseam by all-seeing, unforgiving slow-motion television replays. A Test match umpire who feels he may have made a mistake does not any longer spend the following night wondering how bad it was: he knows exactly how bad it was, cannot escape it and will have it rerun and criticized to an extent that only those of resilient nature can withstand. Small wonder, then, that the innovative United Cricket Board of South Africa thought it desirable, late in 1995, to test their leading umpires for stress, wiring up an attachment to check the regularity of the heartbeat during a Test match day. The resultant graph, when related to the specific pressure points of any given day, will have made a fascinating study, even if it is not necessarily of any practical use.

There have been instances around the world of umpires feeling obliged to give up the job in search of peace of mind because, almost literally, it was driving them mad. That it has happened more frequently in England is due to the volume of cricket played, which elevates umpiring to a full-time profession and imparts to it demands of diligence and quality more rigorous than those elsewhere in the world. It is now a job with promotion prospects, too, for umpires can not only aspire to the first-class panel, and then to the Test match panel, but onwards to the elite group of international umpires, sponsored by the National Grid, who travel the world under the direction

of the International Cricket Council to stand as the 'independent' umpire (the word 'neutral' having been rejected on the
grounds that it suggests impartiality does not apply to all) now
required in Test matches. It is a good development, probably
overdue given the number of series that were blighted by
accusations of 'home-town' umpiring, but it has created its
own problems, for there is an ever-widening gulf in status and
earnings between those at the top of the profession and those
on the shop floor. The pressure to be correct in decision-
making is greater than ever for those in the elite, striving to
sustain a new standard of living, and it is bound to have had
some effect on the traditional relationship between umpires
and players.

Illingworth has no doubts on the matter. 'Umpires were
more friendly in my days as a player because they had fewer
pressures. There were no television replays to bother them
and, if they made a mistake, while it might have been acknowledged by the players concerned, they got away with it publicly.
You got to know them a lot better in those days.'

Gooch agrees: 'Overseas, there is no close relationship
between players and umpires. In my experience, it just doesn't
happen. Here in England, it doesn't occur as much as it once
did because their position and their responsibilities have
changed.' But Dominic Cork, who has never known the way
things used to be, is happy enough with his relationship with
the umpires. 'Someone actually wrote me a letter recently in
which he said I always seemed to be talking to umpires. He
wanted to know if I was abusing them. I'm not, of course, or
I wouldn't have very long in the game. I do talk to them a
good bit, but I'm wise enough to know it would be mad to
try to upset them.'

If, the loquacious Cork apart, umpires communicate less
chummily with the players these days, they are obliged to
communicate more closely with each other. And at the highest
levels this involves not only the two umpires in action on the

field but a third, hidden away behind a window of the pavilion with a television monitor, walkie-talkie and, usually, a match referee for company. Adjudication of Test cricket is no longer a two-man business; neither is it a business which relies on the assessments and instincts of the naked eye and ear. But not everyone is convinced of the merits of technology. The most obvious benefit of the use of TV replays to judge tight line decisions, such as run-outs and stumpings, is that there is no longer any excuse for getting them wrong. The downside is that it breaks up the pace of the game while taking away one more element of the human side of cricket and replacing it with a computer. In an age where the money at stake overrides everything, and where one demonstrably incorrect decision can change so much, the argument against technology has a hollow ring, yet Michael Atherton is one who has put it with passion. 'I accept that umpires are human beings and that they are going to make mistakes, just as batsmen, bowlers, fielders and, of course, captains make mistakes. And I want to keep that human element in the game.' While regretting its introduction, however, Atherton stresses that the technology now available to umpires must be used consistently, a point taken up by Graham Gooch.

I was in favour of the third umpire from the start and nothing has happened since to change my view. But umpires must use it for every tight decision. In Australia, during our 1994−5 tour, Darryll Hair twice decided not to call on the replay for run-out appeals, giving each of them not out. Both were shown to be out when the replay was shown to TV viewers and we suffered on both occasions. I can recall another instance that would have worked the other way. When I was batting at Headingley against Pakistan in 1992, television replays showed I had been run out by all of eighteen inches. The system was not then available to umpires and Kenny Palmer ruled me in. Now that it is available, it must be fully employed, for at least then you are sure to get the right decisions.

Two instances on England's 1995–6 tour of South Africa, both involving Graham Thorpe, demonstrate the obligation of umpires to use the replay system and the inherent risks if they do not. The first was far and away the more dramatic, for it came at a crucial stage of England's second innings in the final Test match at Newlands, Cape Town, when Thorpe was batting well enough to nourish England's hopes of victory. Setting off for a misguided single, Thorpe arrived at the bowler's end so close to the ball breaking the stumps that the naked eye could not accurately separate them. The umpire involved was the South African, Dave Orchard, officiating in only his second Test, and he decided, fatefully, that there was no need for closer inspection. He gave Thorpe not out without referring to his colleague with the TV monitor. This might have passed with no more than muttered doubt but for the fact that South African television, their production not bound by an umpire's discretionary behaviour, immediately ran the incident in slow-motion for the benefit of its viewers. It was clear from this that Thorpe had failed to make his ground – not only to the viewers at home, but to those at Newlands watching it on monitors in the private boxes. Uproar ensued, the message was taken up around the ground and, as the crowd bayed its unmistakable message, Hansie Cronje, the captain of South Africa, approached Orchard demanding that he should reconsider.

Cronje's conduct was technically reprehensible – certainly inasmuch as he approached Thorpe and suggested that he should leave the field – but it was understandable nonetheless. Here he was, on the verge of winning a Test, and with it a series, and a vital, perhaps conclusive wicket was being denied him by the mistaken stubbornness of an umpire. Officially, he was breaking the players' code of conduct in asking for a replay, and he was subsequently fined half his match fee, but Orchard, now painfully aware that he had erred, was in a dilemma. The strong thing to do would have been to stand by his decision and instruct the South Africans to bowl the next ball. Instead, having limply conferred with his on-field colleague, Steve Randell from Australia, who merely confirmed that he was entitled to change his mind, Orchard belatedly surrendered the decision to technology and Thorpe was sent on his way.

This was a classic example of the right decision being reached in the wrong way. The potential ramifications were alarming, for it had now been proved that television's ever-strengthening hold on the game now extended to the power to overrule an umpire. It had also been proved that player power on the field, essentially the bullying of an umpire into changing a decision, could succeed. It was a very sad day for cricket, let alone for England, who had lost before close of play, and it led many to reconsider their support for the third-umpire system.

Thorpe and Cronje were both involved again, a week later, in the second example of an umpire failing to use the available system. The England player took a catch close to the boundary rope during a one-day international. Stepping backwards several paces after catching the ball, he became aware of the rope, stopped, balanced and stared wryly down at the ground behind him. It was a perfectly fair catch, completed inside the line, but the umpire misinterpreted Thorpe's body language and, without consulting him, or referring to the third umpire, awarded a six. Thorpe then frantically signalled that he had caught the ball fairly, the confused umpire sought assistance, and Cronje, showing rare sportsmanship, accepted Thorpe's claim and spared the blushes of the umpire by giving himself out. The possibility of further embarrassment and ill-feeling being created by television replays was thus avoided only by Cronje's good grace.

Gooch is among those who believe that the theory of slo-mo technology could be extended. 'You could wire up the umpires for virtually anything, even for help with lbws, and maybe it will come to that. But the delays this would produce would mean you'd need about eight hours to get through a day's cricket.' Dominic Cork, who is perhaps responsible for more lbw appeals per day than any other bowler in the modern game, is, gratifyingly, of the same view. 'Lbw decisions must continue to be made on the field of play. But the umpires have such a hard job that technology should be used whenever possible if it helps them to get things right.'

The same principle is being applied to scorers, the unseen auditors of the game. It was a giant leap from carving notches on a stick to writing figures in a book, but it has been a monumental one – too great for some of the old retainers of the county circuit – to operate computer screens. It is progress, of course, and there will be no backward steps, just as umpires will never again have to rely exclusively on their own judgement nor batsmen on their ability to prosper without the equivalent of armour plating. All of these are symptoms of the robotic age that is enveloping cricket, enslaving all involved in it to technology. Quite where it will end boggles the mind, for as we have seen, even twenty years ago, the sights and sounds of today's Test cricket, if presented as a vision of the future, would have been ridiculed as fanciful nonsense.

10

The National Interest

Of all the many changes sweeping through the game of cricket
worldwide, none has been more fundamental than the concentration of resources on national teams, if necessary at the
expense of domestic competition. In sport, as in industry,
barriers have come down and untapped opportunities are pre-
senting themselves within an international market. Most
cricketing nations have recognized this. Only England lag
behind.

In Australia, possessors of incontestably the strongest
national cricket team of the 1990s, and in South Africa, a
revelation both on and off the field since their readmittance to
the Test-playing fold in 1991, the leading players are identified,
embraced and encouraged through channels that will benefit
their country above all else. There is no argument about this,
because they are contracted and salaried by their national
boards and employed primarily to play international cricket.
Whatever provincial matches they can accommodate within
these parameters are incidental and discretionary, in a way
entirely alien to the overworked English professional.

If an Australian or South African is carrying a minor injury
during a Test series, or if he is thought simply to be in need
of a break, he will be instructed by the selectors to rest between
major games. It is common sense, a question of looking after

the players who will make the country successful. Yet if an Englishman is in a similar position, he will still be expected to resume the crazy, seven-days-a-week treadmill of county cricket as soon as he steps out of a Test arena, because his wages are paid by his county, not his country. It is no longer good enough to explain away this anomaly on the pretext that England sustains the only full-time professional structure, nor to be proud of it in any arrogant or insular way. Naturally, nobody with the beauties of the game at heart remains unmoved by county cricket, or unwilling to go to great lengths to support its upkeep, but only the blind romantics can now fail to divine that, in England, the cart is being put before the thoroughbreds who should be pulling it.

The England team, and particularly successive captains and managers thereof, have been labouring under a handicap of what might kindly be thought of as apathy in high places but in some cases has transmitted itself as resentment. Small wonder, then, that the last fifteen years of the twentieth century have seen England slip ever further from their once accustomed pre-eminence, spawning annual breastbeating about the state of the English game, quickly replaced by mere hot air once it comes before the decision-makers at Lord's. By 1995, the periodical and notional league tables of Test cricket published by national newspapers told a sorry tale of decline. England could no longer count upon even India, Pakistan and New Zealand, whose teams were once traditionally ground underfoot by even substandard sides from cricket's mother country, to languish beneath them. By some estimates, indeed, only the Johnny-come-latelys Sri Lanka and Zimbabwe could confidently be ranked below England – and there was increasing reason to be unsure of at least one of these.

The English system was devised for a different age, a different game. It was desirable while there was only one county competition and a sensible ration of Test cricket; it remained serviceable for as long as it took opposing nations to catch up, in playing terms, and overtake England in organization and outlook. Nowadays, it is thoroughly untenable, perpetuated by those who confuse their responsibilities to individual counties with their position of power within the game as a whole. Only in England can progress be blocked by vested local interests, by men who come to meetings of the Test and County Cricket Board filled with the indignation of parish councillors utterly unaware of what is taking place beyond their boundaries. Their equivalents in Australia and South Africa laugh at the destructive parochialism of it all, and rightly so, for it does a grave disservice to the players who must produce the results and does much to stifle, rather than nurture, the available talent.

Around the world, too much cricket is being played. Too much international cricket, that is. But only in England is this augmented by a relentless round of county cricket in which there are no concessions to the best and most overworked players. There is a reason for this, of course. It is called the system. The system dictates that the counties, and their delegates, call every shot at decision-making meetings of the Test and County Cricket Board, so that the realistic requirement to create a more competitive, more focused national team are routinely crushed beneath the stampede of local interests, the perceived priority of providing as much county cricket as possible to fill the season. This should not be misinterpreted: the vast majority of delegates to the board act inoffensively, even unwittingly. They are not against the England team; many of them will spend their own money travelling overseas to support them each winter. They believe they are doing their best within their given mandates. But those mandates come, initially, from their individual county committees, who in turn are driven by the short-term, narrow and often petty wishes of their own members. If a proposal arises which would plainly benefit the wellbeing – and consequently, who knows, the performance – of the national team, it will receive automatic rejection if it is deemed to threaten the cosy routines and expectations of those members.

Too harsh? I think not. Even the self-evidently sound extension of preparation time for the England team before home Test matches, when it was proposed in 1990, met some bitter opposition from those who resented the fact that it would dictate the playing days of County Championship fixtures, and that these might not be convenient to all of their members. It was mind-bogglingly small-time, but it was far from being the only example of such damaging insouciance towards the Test team, who are, increasingly, the providers of the game's image and profile, not to mention the vast and growing majority of the English game's revenue, the annual hand-out which keeps most of the counties afloat.

Early in 1989, Ted Dexter was appointed to chair a new body to be known as the England committee. It resembled the traditional selection committee but was to have additional arms to embrace development, preparation and administration. This was undoubtedly an enlightened move, a concession towards the changing times and altered needs. Predictably it was not the brainchild of the TCCB delegates, the county chairmen and chief executives, but of the executive committee and, in particular, of Raman Subba Row, who chaired both that committee and the board itself. Subba Row was already regarded with some suspicion by many board members and his autocratic promotion of Dexter was an incendiary action, confirmation to many that, under his stewardship, the traditional and trusted (if discredited) system of rule by a kind of democratic bureaucracy (a fudge) was being undermined. Dexter, who sprang into his role proclaiming somewhat theatrically, though quite genuinely, his belief that everything he had done in his full and varied life had prepared him for the task, found all too soon that he was not leading a band of willing compatriots to a brighter tomorrow but swimming in a sea of sharks.

Come the summer of 1993, he had had enough. True, his tenure had begun with a public-relations disaster, namely that he had had to proclaim his support for one captain (David Gower) knowing it would eventually be revealed that he had actually wanted to appoint another. Mike Gatting's return to the post was vetoed – in my view, quite correctly – by Ossie Wheatley, the then cricket chairman of the board. Dexter had misjudged the moment and underestimated the mood of justified censure directed towards Gatting for the events that had led to his initial dismissal. Thereafter, Dexter strove to make up lost ground, but the ways in which he did this were largely unseen and widely unappreciated. The initiative for four-day championship cricket was his, and its adoption would have been long delayed without him; the creation of regular A-team and Under-19 tours, the fruits of which are now being harvested, was the work of Dexter and his committee; so, too, was that small but significant matter of gathering the Test team on a Tuesday rather than a Wednesday, the pre-tour training camps at Lilleshall and the introduction of an altogether more thorough system of observing and assessing players. All of this was achieved and Dexter worked harder at his role than any chairman of selectors I have known, sitting on seven different committees and attending upwards of fifty meetings a year to preach the needs of the national team. His ultimate reward was disenchantment, and the indignity of a Test match crowd cheering the radio announcement of his resignation. It was cruel and unfair, and it reflected poorly on those within the TCCB structure who not only failed to support him but, in some subversive cases, deliberately set out to make his position untenable.

Dexter was, and is, a thoroughly engaging man, but his abiding problem is the tendency to make flippant remarks that can be used by those of a mind to discredit him as evidence that he is dotty and therefore unsuitable. This failing helped to bring him down, although eventually he was weary of the unequal battle in any case. Earlier in that summer of 1993, when England were already 2—0 down to Australia, I sat in the passenger seat of Dexter's Jaguar as he drove to Luton to watch Mark Lathwell, the promising Somerset opening batsman (typical of the way things were progressing, he was to be out for nought). Dexter, under pressure on all fronts, reflected upon his perennial handicap.

> I am for ever fighting parochial concerns. After I had been in this job two years, one county chairman banged his fist on the table during a board meeting and said, 'All we seem to do is discuss England.' I thought that was a considerable triumph, but it also told me plenty about what I am up against. I have had to fight my corner two or three times at board level. My committee had only been operating for one year when a motion was tabled to scrap the whole thing. Then they wanted an inquiry into the workings of the England committee, as if we were some dangerous organization.

Dexter widened those expressive eyes and shook his noble head. And well he might. No sooner was he out of the way, later in that series, than moves were underway to wind up the England committee and go back to the old system of selectors. For those from the shires, it had all been too threatening, a group working out of their orbit and, to some degree, out of their control. The England committee, to them, seemed mysteriously single-minded about creating a successful national team and somewhat disinterested in the nitty-gritty of how this might impair the Weston-super-Mare Festival week. It could not be allowed to survive.

Dexter had quietly been pushing England down avenues already explored by Australia, especially in terms of the isolation of the elite players and their eventual employment by a central body. The counties did not like this, either, and to some degree one can understand their reservations. Everything their individual structures had stood for, the pursuit of local success and the gathering of the best team available, was perceived to be at risk if their leading players were to be siphoned off at the whim of the England management. It was a culture shock they could not stomach.

Here, then, is the background to England's undignified decline in the Test nations pecking order. It does not fully explain the poor results of recent years, of course, but it goes a considerable distance towards doing so. After England were beaten by South Africa early in 1996, their problems were aired by one well qualified to know – Bob Woolmer, now South Africa's coach but previously an England Test player and an influential coach in county cricket who might, as I have already suggested, with more foresight from those in the ivory towers, have been enlisted to help his own country rather than an opponent. Woolmer believed that there was talent aplenty in English cricket. 'I think it is more to do with how the players are looked after, how they could better be encouraged into a positive approach,' he said. It was a coded expression of scorn for England's backward ways of dealing with the protection and promotion of their most precious assets.

Those players themselves occasionally glance with envy at the treatment of their counterparts abroad. This was especially evident in Australia during the 1994–5 tour, when Shane Warne, Craig McDermott and David Boon were all instructed to rest between Tests rather than playing for their states in what, by English standards, is the very brief and streamlined Sheffield Shield. They knew it could not and would not happen in England. Not yet, anyway. For England is currently engaged in the process of wearing down its best players, burning out their passion, mental and physical, and shortening their careers. Dominic Cork and Darren Gough, the two brightest stars to shine from this country in recent years, will both be affected; indeed they are already feeling the pressure. Gough felt obliged to play for Yorkshire during the summer of 1995 when the advice and urgings from the England camp were that he should rest an injury. And Cork, as wholehearted a trier as one could wish to find, confesses: 'There is too much county cricket. I think we should cut down on the amount of four-day and one-day games.'

His voice has not yet been heard. Many others have cried out on this theme in vain. Dexter, in the throes of battle on yet another club-versus-country issue and still trying to persuade the malcontents of the virtues of four-day cricket, said, with splendid exasperation, to the TCCB delegates: 'You can play cricket on skates if you want to, so long as you give me one proper competition.' He finally got his way on that one, but there is no sign of a slackening of pace in the domestic season, for all the warning signs. Graeme Wright, when editor of *Wisden*, wrote prophetically in the 1991 edition of the problems of the English structure and its regressive effect on international prospects.

> Perhaps the plateau [of county cricket] should be smaller, making the competition for places on it greater. For this to happen, the structure of county cricket would have to change. And while, at present, it is inconceivable that the first-class counties would agree to any such change, it is possible that the coming years will show change to be inevitable. A lot will depend on how English cricket views its role on the small stage of international cricket: a star performer or a player of supporting parts.

There is the nub. The game is now an international one, expanding all the time. If Ali Bacher, the visionary, missionary figure at the helm of South African cricket, could have his global wish, there would be sixteen Test-playing countries by early in the twenty-first century. Then, of course, the best cricketers would be fully employed playing for their countries. In the meantime, with only nine in the field, England's best must continue to perform mental and physical contortions to attempt to serve their twin employers, probably doing justice to neither.

Raymond Illingworth has witnessed the years of revolution in the profile of Test cricket at closer quarters than most. While he shares the concerns of the players about their workload, and struggles in vain to revive the seeds planted by Dexter and establish a system of central contracts for leading players, he emphasizes the altered status of the England team since his playing days. He is thinking not just of the attention and expectations foisted upon them but, inevitably, of the available rewards. Raymond is a Yorkshireman, after all. 'I was paid £125 for my first Test in 1958 and I only received twice that amount, even as captain, the last time I played, fifteen years later,' he relates with the grumpiness of one intimately aware that the modern England player, even the most junior of recruits to the Test side, could now expect to pocket close to £3,000 per game. 'When I went to Australia as captain for the 1970–1 tour,' he went on, 'I was given £25 as captain's expenses. I still don't know what it was supposed to cover, but when we got to Heathrow I put it on the bar and told the lads to get themselves a drink.' It is the idea of Illingworth brandishing cash at a bar rather than the parsimony of his expense account that is more likely to raise eyebrows. Clearly, some things have changed more than others.

Graham Gooch played international cricket for even longer than Illingworth and his career took in the financial revolution of 1977, when the incursions of Kerry Packer roused the defences of English cricket and Cornhill Insurance mounted a profound and sustainable rescue package, through which the match fee for a new Test player was instantly swelled from

£210 to £1,000. It has risen steadily ever since, and Gooch, slightly surprised at his own recollections, tells how his first, ill-fated Test match in 1975 earned him £200 and his last on home territory, at the Oval nineteen years later, more than £4,000.

Equally striking, however, are the memories of both men regarding the build-up to their Test debuts in relation to modern-day preparations. Illingworth was called up for the Old Trafford Test against New Zealand in July 1958 – oddly enough, the same match in which Ted Dexter made his England debut. England were to win the match by an innings, just as they had done the previous two games, and in the manner in which they were accustomed to dealing with their opponents, who, with the traditional exception of Australia, were generally starkly inferior. These were the days when the international circuit was largely uncompetitive, when Ashes series were all that truly mattered, and when England's pre-eminence around the cricketing world was still to be properly challenged. They were also the days when the pre-match atmosphere was conspicuously relaxed, indeed comparatively casual, when set against the modern routines.

'We would all have been playing for our counties until the Tuesday evening, so we didn't meet up at the Test venue until after lunch on the Wednesday,' recalls Illingworth. 'We were supposed to arrive before three o'clock but even when we got there it was all very gentle compared to the practice sessions the teams of today go through. The bowlers had probably bowled plenty of overs for their counties and would not be keen to do much in the nets. There was never much attention paid to fielding, either. And there was no media attention. It was rare to see a journalist before the morning of the match.'

The media focus was growing by the time Gooch first played for England, against the 1975 Australians. As he was an unworldly twenty-one-year-old, unprepared in virtually every way for the ordeal, it is not an experience he looks back upon with any pleasure. This is partly though not exclusively because England, caught on an uncovered pitch soaked by a storm, were beaten by an innings inside four days and because Gooch began what was to be an illustrious and elongated Test career with a 'pair'. But his distress went deeper than that.

> I didn't feel welcome. Although the game was at Edgbaston, we stayed about twenty miles away, in the Raven Hotel at Droitwich, and after the team dinner on the Wednesday evening I slipped into the callbox to phone my mum before following the usual Essex routine and strolling into the bar. I was amazed to find nobody there and I stood around at a loss, wondering if they had all gone out without me, or if I was supposed to be in bed. Nobody had spoken to me, you see, and I just didn't know what was expected. Throughout that game I never once felt part of the unit and on Sunday, which was a rest day, I drove all the way home to Essex for some of my mum's chips. Next morning, back in Droitwich, I saw some of the senior players loading their suitcases into their car boots. They had decided that we were going to lose the game a day early and that they could go home that night. It had never occurred to me to be so fatalistic.

Naïve though Gooch perhaps was, his story is nevertheless an example of the absence of communication that can afflict and weaken a Test side. Ironically, Gooch himself was accused of this failing on more than one occasion during his tenure as captain two decades later. Mark Lathwell was one player who claimed he had never been made to feel a part of Gooch's team. Although not a naturally gregarious or talkative man, Gooch did care a great deal about the side at his command

and one of his ongoing arguments with Dexter, chairman throughout his time as captain, was that Dexter did not spend sufficient time in the dressing room acquainting himself with the players and their needs. Dexter resisted the plea, explaining: 'I shouldn't be too close to the players. When we win, you haven't seen me around. I tend to turn up when there is a bit of firefighting to be done.' And so, stoical to the end, he did, but the feeling among the players remained one of uncomfortable distance, an atmosphere not helped by an embarrassing incident prior to the Fifth Test against Australia in 1993. Gooch had just resigned, the Ashes once again lost, and Michael Atherton had taken over as captain. He had just concluded his team talk in the dressing room when Dexter appeared to spread a little encouragement and bonhomie. Casting his eyes around the room, he approached a lean, dark-haired individual and wished him luck with the new ball. Dexter had taken him for Martin Bicknell, who had just been recalled to the side. Unfortunately, he had bestowed his good wishes upon the team physiotherapist, Dave Roberts.

Before the game had ended, Dexter had resigned – not because of that incident, though it was redolent of its time. His successor, Raymond Illingworth, approached the job in an entirely different way. Far from distancing himself from the players, he could not be kept out of the dressing room and this, inevitably, led to a conflict with the team manager, Keith Fletcher, which was precisely what Dexter had been so anxious to avoid. There simply was not room for both Fletcher and Illingworth in an intimate, decision-making role close to the team. Fletcher's dismissal following the Australian tour of 1994–5, though sudden and somewhat unexpected, was a merciful release from the purgatory of confused control within which Atherton and his players were striving to operate.

The dual role of chairman and manager was specifically created to suit Illingworth. It acknowledged that his presence in authority would otherwise be divisive, for he is not a man

to defer to others when decisions need taking. It also acknowledged the general view that he must be allowed his head,
allowed to prove what he had always claimed, that he was the
man best qualified to manage the fortunes of the Test team.
And, despite the hiccup of another overseas defeat in South
Africa the following winter, Illingworth did create within the
team a positive and united feel that spoke well of his closeness
to the players and their respect for him. However, the age-old
problem of managing a disparate group – that this applied to
most of the players but not quite all – did rear its head. Early
on the tour of South Africa, much was made of criticism
directed at Devon Malcolm by Illingworth and his appointed
bowling coach, Peter Lever. The management had made
efforts to adjust Malcolm's action; Malcolm rebelled against
it, so the management called him names. Messy all round.
Back in England, Malcolm received widespread sympathy, not
only because he is a popular figure but because there was a
feeling that he should be an automatic choice in the Test side.
This theory was not borne out by the overwhelming balance
of his form at England level but human nature dictates that
people remember such things as his 9 for 57 on a scorching
summer Saturday at the Oval while forgiving and forgetting
much else. Malcolm was a hero; ergo, Illingworth was an
ogre. The issue simmered all tour and came to an unpleasant
head when Malcolm, released from his duties prior to the
one-day series that concluded the itinerary, wasted no time in
giving a series of newspaper 'exclusives' in which the dominant
subject was his alleged mistreatment by the management. He
even wondered, in print, whether Illingworth would have
treated a white cricketer in such a way, though this unworthy
and unwarranted suggestion was subsequently withdrawn.

Those who were in South Africa, either within the team
or close to it, saw the affair in somewhat different light. Illingworth and Lever had discussed the proposed remedial work
with Malcolm even before the tour party was announced, and

they claim Malcolm was willing and enthusiastic. When the time came for action, however, he was uncooperative. Illingworth tried the carrot and then reverted, possibly crudely, to the stick. Deliberately and calculatingly, he insulted Malcolm in an effort to goad him into action. It was a crass misjudgement of a man far more likely to sulk in such circumstances and this, by all accounts, is what he did. Late in the tour, he was recalled for the final Test at Cape Town and whatever confidence in him Atherton retained vanished during a spell with the second new ball so stray and tame, so contrarily at odds with the output of any self-respecting strike bowler that it beggared belief. It also went a long way to costing England the match and the series. Malcolm went home, tail between legs, to tell his tales of prejudice and persecution. The moral of this story is that no matter how many managers and coaches are attached to a team, and how assiduously they address the matter of man-management, it can still go dreadfully, damagingly wrong.

When the England squad convened for their first international event of the 1995 summer, the Texaco Trophy one-day series against West Indies, they encountered Illingworth in a guise he had not adopted while merely chairman. He wore a tracksuit, which he subsequently peeled off to exercise his sixty-two-year-old joints with a gentle over of nostalgic off-breaks. Moreover, he was accompanied by three more tracksuited figures – John Edrich to assist the batsmen, Lever the bowlers and Alan Knott the wicketkeepers. Here was a team of expert coaches and aides busying themselves in a way that would have been quite unfamiliar to, and possibly resented by, the Test teams of old – as unfamiliar, indeed, as the intensive net session and hectic fielding routines that the players were then put through under Illingworth's avuncular gaze. There was a precision to the session that augured well and Atherton, the captain, sensed it. His understandable reservations about the power now invested in Illingworth, and where it might leave him, began to recede.

A month later, he was not so sure. A month later, Illingworth used all the considerable power that had been put at his disposal and acted in a unilateral fashion probably unprecedented on the eve of a major Test match. The England team, chosen as usual by Illingworth, Atherton and two other selectors, had gathered at Lord's, and its balance and strategy had been decided and publicly announced when Illingworth decided to alter it. He sent home the chosen wicketkeeper, Steve Rhodes, and reimposed the gloves on an ambivalent and somewhat confused Alec Stewart. One selector, at least, was neither consulted nor best pleased, while Atherton was left to put a phlegmatic public front on what he privately considered a serious undermining of his authority. That England won the match, gloriously, was incidental to the issue, though not to management harmony. Here was someone carrying his influence to the limit and risking a souring of his working relationship with the man who will always be primarily accountable, the man who must take the team on the field and make it work: the captain.

Arguments have raged for years now about the value or otherwise of team managers at international level but, while their brief and roles will vary, they are not going to disappear. The days when a panel of selectors picked a team and handed it over to the charge of the captain are irrecoverably gone. The profile of the international game now insists that a captain needs support of the kind provided by Bob Woolmer in South Africa and, over a long period, by Bob Simpson in Australia. Whether there will, or should, ever again be such a dominant off-field figure as Illingworth, however, remains to be seen.

It was in 1899 that a single selection committee first picked England's teams for a complete series, the job having hitherto been conducted by the MCC committee for matches at Lord's and by the host county committee elsewhere. And it was in 1964 that no less a figure than Field-Marshal Montgomery of Alamein wrote a letter to E. W. Swanton of the *Daily Telegraph* deploring the practice. 'I would abolish the selectors,' wrote the field-marshal. 'With a group of that sort, all having different opinions, the final result will always be a compromise – and that is the beginning of failure, the way to lose battles. Let the captain chose his own team.'

The opposite viewpoint, that which would give the captain no say whatever in selection, is dearer to some hearts and operates in theory, if not in practice, in Australia. My opinion is that a captain ought never to be divorced from the selection of the side he must command (and neither of the last two Australian captains, Allan Border and Mark Taylor, have been without a substantial voice) but that, no matter who picks the team, the same principles apply. Win, and the players are heroes; lose, and the selectors are fools.

It was after the Lord's Test of 1993, during the press conference at which his frivolous comment about planets being in the wrong juxtaposition was mischievously taken as further ammunition with which to lampoon him, that Ted Dexter made a somewhat more profound statement about selection. 'I simply don't know if we as selectors have made mistakes,' he said in answer to a searching question about his culpability. 'It is always assumed when someone plays badly that someone else would have played better. We just don't know if that is the case. They may have done worse. They may have done the same. As a selector you are permanently debating these things.'

As with selection, so with team management, and so with the playing itself – everything connected with the England Test team has now been inflated in importance. Competition around the world has intensified and the game has aspired to a prominent place in the entertainment marketplace of the late twentieth century. What it means is that the relaxed routines of the days when Illingworth began his Test cricket are but a distant memory. The available rewards, attainable standards of living, competitive environment and ever-increasing demands of professionalism conspire to make international cricket an arena reserved for the strong of body and mind. Graham Gooch, reflecting on an England career just ended, put it into perspective.

> The pressure to succeed at the highest level is far higher now than when I started out because the profile of the game is so much greater. For an international player there is a great deal of cricket, probably far too much. This can put a great strain on family life but the hardest bit is mentally sustaining the peaks necessary to succeed. Every time you approach a match you have to go through so many processes. It never does get any easier.

And probably it never will, certainly not in England for as long as those who decide such matters blindly fill up the calendar and, by so doing, decline all safeguards for the future of the star player.

In the spring of 1996 Raymond Illingworth resigned part of his joint commission with the England team and stood down as team manager, the duties passing to the Lancashire coach, David Lloyd. It was Illingworth's way of admitting that it was time for a younger outlook. It was also an admission that he had tried to change things, and failed.

11

Media: The Power and the Threat

When Michael Atherton arrived home from South Africa early in 1996, having spent more than three months overseas and having suffered a good deal of disappointment, he strode through the Heathrow Airport terminal pushing his trolley, a case of South African wine perched atop his suitcase, and declined to speak to anyone. Those he ignored included a phalanx of newspaper and broadcast-media reporters, many of whom appeared offended by this rebuff from the England captain. They had come expecting him to spend time with them, to explain why England had lost both the Test series and the one-day series, to dissect the past and predict the future. They did not know their man. Retreating, indignant, they labelled him Captain Grumpy and some, doubtless, decided that he was no longer the man for the job.

Yet what could Atherton have said? And why should he have said anything? For the previous fortnight, ever since England had plunged to defeat in the final Test in Cape Town before embarking on an ill-conceived round of limited-overs games, he had been conducting interviews, struggling to give explanations, striving to impart some hope for the World Cup that was to follow. In his own mind, he had obliged every representative of the touring cricket media and now, with a mere ten days at home before repacking the suitcase and heading off to Pakistan, he did not regard dawn at Heathrow as the time or the place to restate his thoughts on the state of the English game. He considered that he had said all there was to say and that, therefore, his duties were suspended.

So who was right – the news media for expecting an exhausted England captain to make himself available for platitudinous and repetitive interviews on stepping off a homebound flight, or Atherton for thinking it beyond the call of duty? There is no definitive answer to this, for it is just one minor yet typical example of the trend that has overtaken cricket, just as it did football, a trend in the media that demands quotes, or soundbites, no matter how anodine they may be and no matter what an imposition it is to the mouthpiece concerned. The comments are then used to create headlines, in either broadcasting or newspaper terms, and to provoke reaction from other involved parties – hence more quotes, more soundbites, more headlines, more reaction. And so the circle continues.

It is all so far removed from the long-standing traditions of reporting cricket as to be unrecognizable. The question, however, is whether the game and its players have benefited. On the plus side they receive incalculably more coverage than of old, which not only raises the profile of the game as a whole but can dramatically promote individuals to prominence. The debits are a lack of privacy – for intrusion affects famous cricketers as well as stars of soap opera and, not to be confused with them, members of the royal family – and a lack of perspective, reflected in the inclination of areas of the media to create 'astonishing rows' out of purely mundane happenings. The game, and its major players, is now constantly under scrutiny and receives the column inches to match. It is helping to make cricket financially rich but whether, as a result, its human relations are all the poorer is a matter for debate.

Atherton, a man who values his privacy, detests being photographed and finds it hard to adopt artificial moods for media purposes, provides two further case studies. In the summer of 1994, he was an embattled man and it was largely his own fault. Under suspicion of ball-tampering during the Lord's Test match against South Africa, he admitted that he had lied to the match referee about precisely what (dirt, as it transpired) was in his infamous trouser pocket. Now, very few outside observers had the first idea what it was he was alleged to have done with the dirt, or what possible advantage he could have gained (probably none, even if it had been in his mind to try), but the drama of the situation, the admission that he had compromised his integrity, set off an almighty brouhaha. For a week, speculation was to rage about whether Atherton would resign from the captaincy or whether, indeed, he should be sacked. It became a hysterical witch-hunt and the perspectives of the situation were long forgotten, along with any respect for the sanctity of a man's home.

Atherton, returning to his flat in Didsbury, near Manchester, after his chastening weekend had ended with a lost match and a £2,000 fine, discovered he had company. A clutch of news reporters were waiting outside, ready to badger him into an indiscretion in the same way that they would wait on the doorsteps of sexually erring politicians. Atherton fled, taking his girlfriend to the Lake District and a pub where he was confident he would be free to relax and think. But this was not an inviolable bolthole either; his presence was discovered and the pack closed in again. Eventually Atherton stayed in three different hotels on consecutive nights before emerging to hold a press conference at which he confirmed that he would be continuing in the job. What he did not say then was that as he questioned if it was all worthwhile, the time he had come closest to resigning – a decision that would have been calamitous for English cricket – was when he realized that he could not even go home in peace. Was this onslaught justified by the convenient pretext that he was a public figure? Or was it the crude hounding of a distinguished and popular sportsman?

Chris Balderstone officiates as third umpire, responsible for adjudicating on TV replays, during the 1993 Lord's Test match. *(G. Morris)*

Graham Gooch obliges a gathering of journalists and hangers-on with his views on India, 1993. *(P. Eagar)*

There was a time when the toss was a private ritual, conducted simply between the opposing captains. Now it is a television circus. (P. Eagar)

Overseas players from the 1970s
and the 1990s, both candidates for
the distinction of being the best
batsman of modern times – Barry
Richards, *left*, of Hampshire and
South Africa and Brian Lara, *below*,
of Warwickshire and West Indies.
(P. Eagar)

More than 100,000 people turned up for the technological shambles that was the 1996 World Cup opening ceremony, a prime case of wasted money. (*Allsport*)

A year later, re-established in the captaincy without serious challenge, Atherton was distraught at the circumstances surrounding England's seven-session defeat against West Indies at Edgbaston, and said as much in a number of articulate interviews. The pitch, he said, was the worst on which he had ever played Test cricket. It was 'diabolical'. This, one would have thought, was a strong enough line, certainly for those journalists whose brief was cricket above scandal, but in the ensuing days Atherton found that, no matter what the mitigating circumstances, a beaten England captain is a soft target for tabloid abuse and that if his home was not a haven, then neither was his dressing room. He was changing in his usual position in the Lancashire pavilion at Old Trafford during a one-day game that followed the Edgbaston fiasco. The room is on the first floor and has a picture-window frontage. From the far side of the ground, through a powerful long lens, a freelance photographer captured Atherton in the act of changing his trousers. He sold the picture to the *Sun*, who gleefully plastered the bare backside of the England captain on their back page under the headline 'SILLY ARSE'. The defence is that this is opportunist journalism (I doubt if even anyone at the *Sun* could claim it was in 'the public interest'); the truth is that it was shabby and unscrupulous. Atherton, angered at what he considered yet another invasion of his territory, consulted his solicitor while Lancashire went to the trouble of blacking out the window that had seen long and hitherto uncontroversial service.

There is no definitive year, much less moment, when the media approach to cricket and cricketers was so comprehensively transformed. It began gradually, insidiously, during the 1970s with the rise of tabloid newspapers and their clamour for quotes-led news stories in preference to match reportage, yet well before this there were occasional instances of players 'telling all' to a newspaper and being well paid for their trouble. The rivalry between the *Sun* and the *Daily Mirror* spawned sensationalism, personally slanted in a way that cricket had not previously experienced. The trend was granted fresh impetus in the late 1970s by the glamorization of the game achieved by Kerry Packer (for whatever else he did to the game, he unarguably bestowed glamour upon it), and it accelerated through the next decade. Now, late in the 1990s, international cricket (and it is important to distinguish that it is only international cricket) carries with it a formidable media entourage.

England has by far the largest number of travelling newspaper journalists, sometimes upward of thirty, accompanying the Test team abroad, but everywhere that the game is played at a high level is now subject to the moulding influence of television. Match schedules are arranged to suit it and games are sometimes delayed so that technicians can sprint on to fix faulty microphones placed in stumps. Television pays the money and calls the shots. This is never more apparent than during the pre-match hour, when reports on everything from pitch conditions to expected weather are transmitted from the middle before the toss is conducted in what can only be described as a media scrum. Once upon a time, and not so very long ago, this was a pleasing ritual with which to begin a game, the captains walking out together from the pavilion and standing in isolation on the square. Nowadays, its ceremony has been abandoned in favour of trailing camera wires, myriad microphones and any number of ex-players in their new guise as television commentators, at least one of whom might actually be there for the purpose of interviewing the captains rather than indulging in chummy small talk with them.

I hesitate to think what that remarkable sportsman-cum-journalist C. B. Fry would have made of it all. Back in the early 1930s, he was working for the London *Evening Standard* as a cricket columnist. In his autobiography, *Life Worth Living*, he describes what may then have been a typical day 'at the office'. 'The press box [at Worcester] was then in the little stand behind the bowler's arm at the New Road end, and here we were installed with Brooks, the chauffeur, stationed just below, at ground level and within easy reach, handy for the dispensing of champagne from the large hamper in his charge.'

Among Fry's press-box colleagues within that idyllic scene was E. W. Swanton. It was the best part of half a century later when that esteemed correspondent of the *Daily Telegraph* described, in an article for the *Cricketer* magazine, how the approach of the cricket writer, indeed of the sportswriter in general, had altered during his career. 'The fact is that comparisons, though not exactly odious, are irrelevant, for the correspondent, whatever the game, has nowadays so many facets to contend with which simply did not obtrude until one popular sport after another became increasingly enmeshed by big money and the need to chase it in order to survive.'

It has, however, not only been the sports who have chased money (latterly, most specifically, through binding but lucrative television deals), but the individual player as well. Here, too, the media have been the providers and the outcome has often been bad feeling and hypocrisy. As long ago as 1958, when Yorkshire were still embroiled in the kind of in-fighting which, Raymond Illingworth avers, prevented them from fulfilling their true potential, Johnny Wardle, a great spin bowler if a controversial character, terminated his own career by writing a series of incendiary articles for the *Daily Mail*. Wardle, having just been informed that his county would not be requiring his services the following season (a reflection on his personality rather than his playing ability) was intensely critical of his captain, Ronnie Burnet, fellow players and the club committee. Yorkshire dismissed him immediately and, in what became something of a cause célèbre, his invitation for the MCC party for the Ashes trip to Australia that winter was withdrawn. The postscripts were rich in irony: Wardle went to Australia anyway, as a columnist for the *Daily Mail*, and Yorkshire's torrid season ended with a fire which destroyed, would you believe it, the Headingley press box. 'Most unfortunate,' said *Wisden* in sober understatement.

The presence of Wardle, still a prominent cricketer, in the press box throughout that series was a sign of things to come. Simultaneously, a more profound change was being wrought. When Ian Craig, the captain of Australia, contracted hepatitis, his job passed to Richie Benaud. Unlike most novice captains, Benaud had very definite ideas about how he wished to change things and one of his priorities was to improve the previously uncommunicative relationship between the Australian players and press. He had a distinct advantage in achieving this aim as he was already a practising journalist and, two years earlier, had taken a television course with the BBC in London, the long-term outcome of which is now well known to all. During that winter of 1958–9, Benaud made a point, a mould-breaking point, of inviting the cricket press into the dressing room at the end of the day's play and conducting his own press conference. It was a move regarded with grave suspicion by some in the England camp, who believed Benaud was trying to gain an unearned psychological bonus, but it was undoubtedly the forerunner of the formalized press conferences which now follow each day's Test cricket around the world.

Benaud has continued to be a prime mover in breaking down the traditional taboos of the media approach to cricket and, as a highly respected television presenter, both for the commercial Channel 9 network in Australia and the BBC in England, he is in a uniquely influential position. Despite writing regularly for tabloid newspapers in both countries, Benaud is by no stretch of the imagination a sensationalist, but within his sound and usually positive style there has always been scope for criticism of players who, in his view, are neglecting their media responsibilities.

Early in 1994, there was an unsavoury incident during Australia's Test match against South Africa in Johannesburg. Merv

Hughes and Shane Warne were both guilty of irrational on-pitch outbursts, in Warne's case directed at the retreating and utterly blameless back of the gentle South African opener Andrew Hudson, whom he had just dismissed. Channel 9's coverage of the match, beamed back live to Australia, was rightly intolerant of such behaviour and was not coy about showing it in full. Subsequently, David Boon, the Australian batsman, wrote an article for his home-town newspaper in Tasmania criticizing Channel 9 for showing close-ups of Warne and Hughes – in other words, for fanning the flames of the affair. Benaud was unsympathetic. Responding in his book *The Appeal of Cricket*, he said that Boon's ideas, 'taken to their logical conclusion, could have all cricket covered with a long lens'. He amplified: 'One of the prime points at issue is that cricketers should always believe whatever they do on the cricket field is being recorded for posterity. To believe otherwise is simply to be naïve.'

Benaud's point is relevant to Atherton and the dirt-in-pocket affair, for to imagine that the England captain would be so obvious and clumsy in any attempt at ball-tampering under the discretionary gaze of any number of TV and stills cameras is to insult his intelligence. And yet, in recent years, cricketers from all countries have forgotten the presence of the all-seeing eye on any number of occasions: remember the stream of obscenities Chris Broad let forth, apparently straight into a homing TV camera, following a dismissal at Lord's? It cannot be easy, within the intensity of modern Test cricket, to reserve even a portion of the brain to warn of the need for constant vigilance, as a brake on anything that could be considered unseemly. It would be a departure from the human responses that cricketers, along with everyone else, have indulged in since time immemorial.

Raymond Illingworth befriended the media when he became England captain. Learning, perhaps, from Benaud, for whose captaincy he had an abiding regard, Illingworth made a habit of being open with the press, both at home and on tour. Sometimes, particularly by less liberal figures of management, he was considered indiscreet, but there were few travelling cricket writers in those days and hardly any who were interested in angling stories to belittle prominent figures — the build-them-up-and-knock-them-down syndrome of the modern sport–media relationship. Illingworth found that he could get the media on his side with this approach and when, after some years working with Benaud at BBC Television, he returned to the England team as chairman of selectors, he fell back into a similar pattern. But the rules had changed, and Illingworth found his fingers being consistently burned as remarks he had blithely considered to be informal guidance and off-the-record cogitating were transformed into headlines, often putting him at odds with his own players and management. At first indignant and vengeful, in time Illingworth came to realize that it was no longer such a simple business to manipulate the media, for now it had many and varied branches, some of them malign.

Cricketers on tour have also found their relations with the press deteriorating sharply to the extent that they harbour an unfairly jaundiced view of all journalists. This never used to be the way of it, not even in the mid-1970s when I undertook my first overseas tour. I was twenty-two years old and the assignment of covering a full Test tour of India, followed by a stop-off in Sri Lanka en route to the Centenary Test in Australia, had been made possible by that grand old man of Fleet Street the late Reg Hayter, whose agency I had joined the previous year. As was the custom for anyone who was employed by Reg, the workload was severe but for an aspiring cricket writer, it was a precious opportunity. My principal problem, on arriving in the pink city of Jaipur a fortnight into the tour, was that I knew hardly any of the England players. I need not have worried. Within a matter of weeks, I counted several of them as friends and, while some of the old stagers treated me with a healthy suspicion until I had proved myself worthy of their trust, there was throughout that trip a sense of camaraderie between the players and the ten or a dozen newspapermen accompanying them. Nights out, sometimes riotously funny and exuberant, were shared without journalists abusing the privilege to write snide stories or players living in fear of it. Until then, I am told, this had been the norm, the way in which players and press co-existed, but it was a happy state of affairs with which I had all too brief a liaison. No tour I have covered since then has had the same feeling attached to it; for that, perhaps the fact that Kerry Packer bought up most of the world's leading cricketers immediately after the Centenary Test must take the greatest share of the blame. Suddenly, there were unprecedented sums of money on offer to players. Suddenly, too, the game was front-page as well as back-page news. Gone for ever was the gentle, civilized life-style of the traditional cricket correspondent.

John Lever was my closest friend among the players on that unforgettable baptismal tour. For him, too, it was a first tour and, I sense, a best tour, one on which he enjoyed an atmosphere that could never be recaptured. Years later, having played with distinction for England and Essex in an unblemished career, he wrote in his autobiography about the changed mood between players and press.

> What has caused so many problems for the England players in more recent years is that, whereas we were only accompanied by bona fide cricket correspondents who had the interests of the game at heart and with whom we shared a mutual respect and a common interest in keeping each other sane, nowadays touring teams are pursued by a press corps containing far more newsmen than genuine cricket writers, who are interested only in finding a story – and the juicier the better.

No cricketer stimulated such an approach, or suffered from it, more than Ian Botham. He could be considered unlucky to have been a star in the age when ability earned no licence from the media, only intensified scrutiny, but for the way he lived his life, not to mention the style in which he played his cricket, Botham was always destined to become a favourite plaything of the press. The sadness, for his many admirers, was that as the attention grew more unflattering and his conduct more dubious, he adopted a show of sanctimony, blaming the media for all his troubles, and one of hypocrisy in unthinkingly taking substantial sums of money from a newspaper who printed more sensational stories about him than any other.

Botham contributed a weekly, ghost-written column for the *Sun* during the headiest days of his career. In 1979, his friend and England colleague Bob Willis had advised him to sever the tie, believing that Botham was compromising himself. Botham's answer was simple: 'My attitude was that the money was good and that no one took the tabloids seriously anyway.' He was kidding himself, of course. As the nature of the Botham stories became more unpleasant, true or false, nobody took them more seriously than Botham himself. He claimed 'character assassination' at the hands of the media; infamously, one night on his then home ground in Somerset, he hurled a deckchair through the window of the Taunton press box. His instinct was to deny, ever more heatedly, whatever was written about him, no matter whether it involved sex, drugs, drink, violence or, very occasionally, cricket. He was the ultimate example of a star turned sour by the new-generation media treatment of cricket. The greatest irony, of course, is that in his avuncular retirement, he now has a column in England for the *Daily Mirror*, in South Africa for the *Sunday Times* and a long-term television commentary contract with Sky Television.

Alongside Botham in the Sky commentary box sit two more former England captains whose relations with the media were often stormy, Bob Willis and David Gower. Willis's playing days were not marked by Bothamesque off-field scandal, but this did not guarantee him an easy ride in media terms. He was not a natural communicator – in fact he was the most engagingly insular cricketer I have ever met – and his instinctive scorn for the ways of the tabloids was exacerbated by their treatment of Botham, for whom he felt a fierce, protective loyalty. When, at Headingley in 1981, Willis followed up Botham's monumental century against Australia by taking 8 for 43 to win one of the most extraordinary Tests of all time, he astonished awestruck television viewers by using his celebratory interview to launch a savage attack on Fleet Street. He talked to me about it while preparing his autobiography, *Lasting the Pace.*

> It probably seemed a graceless act at best, yet I have no special regrets about it. The issue was one on which I felt so strongly that it soured my appreciation of a marvellous win and a notable personal milestone. If I made a mistake it was in not being specific enough about the subject of my resentment . . . There are journalists for whom I have tremendous respect and admiration . . . there are some I like and trust, some I like but don't trust, a few I trust but don't like . . . and then there are those I can neither trust nor like.

Willis's wrath was initially roused by the media treatment of Botham's fall from grace as England captain.

> My anger was directed at the clutch of writers who seemed intent on making utterly untenable the position of England captain. Life had been made hard for Botham in his latter Tests as leader. The very writers who had been boldly campaigning for him

to be given the job not many months earlier were now cruelly consigning him to the rubbish patch. When Mike Brearley came back to take over, I kidded myself that things might be quieter for a while, but his first match back as skipper had not even begun when the *Sun* ran a back-page headline along the lines of 'TEST WAR'. The reason for this slice of melodrama was that Brearley had mentioned he would be protesting if Dennis Lillee went on with his practice of leaving the field to change his shirt between bowling spells. No more, no less. Hardly the stuff for which wars are fought, I would have imagined. Other similar stories were printed around that time which can have had no other motive than mischief-making and, for better or worse, I blew my top about it.

But Willis, too, sacrificed the moral high ground and fell into the hypocrisy trap by, later that same evening, accepting payment from the *Sun* for an exclusive interview. He accepts his mistake. 'It might not have been so bad had it been any other paper, but the *Sun*, in my opinion, has taken cricket reporting further into the "quotes-and-news" area, and further away from basic match reporting, than any of its rivals. I was foolish, and I have been reminded of it by friends and foes in the press contingent whenever I have criticized their profession.'

Gower, at least superficially, is a less intense man than Willis and, during his first spell as England captain his relaxed, informal approach with the press was widely appreciated. Things were different, however, when he returned in 1989. Having taken serious offence when a close journalist friend of his told his readers that Gower was in need of 'a full-frontal lobotomy', he acted entirely out of his perceived character by first walking out of a packed press conference on the Saturday of the Lord's

Test match and then banging his head on a desk, Basil Fawlty-style, in rage at the line of questioning during a conference at Edgbaston. If it could get to Gower, so the general assumption went, it could get to anyone.

Certainly, the media pressure had got to Mike Gatting, who led England with mixed success in the years between Gower's two spells in the job. Gatting had some admirable qualities as a Test captain but articulacy was not among them and nor, sometimes, was common sense. He overslept in Melbourne during the highly successful 1986–7 tour, missing the start of a match against Victoria; the team management made ineffectual attempts to cover up the captain's blunder but Gatting was crucified in print. It hurt him. He had realized early on that he would find media relations difficult and had consulted, among others, his friend Gower. 'David told me I should never take the harsh words of uninformed critics to heart,' he said later. 'Easy to say, not so easy to carry out.' Gatting did not carry it out with style. Often he conducted his press conferences as if he would rather be anywhere else, staring into space or, on one occasion, reading a magazine. It did not go down well with the assembled media, fond of him though many were. And so, as the euphoria of winning in Australia was replaced by the harsh reality of losing at home to Pakistan, Gatting suffered. When he put Pakistan into bat at Edgbaston, he was greeted the following morning by some of the most gratuitously offensive headlines any cricket match can have carried. 'GATT THE PRAT' and 'CAP'N COCK-UP' were but two examples. It was the start of his slide from favour, a slide he himself accelerated beyond measure by his aggression towards the Pakistani umpire Shakoor Rana. After that, his position was untenable and it was eventually as sad for him as it was for the game itself that he kept it long enough for a fatuous story about a dalliance with a barmaid to give the selectors the courage to do what they should have done earlier and dismiss him. Gatting, inevitably, blamed the media, and the scandal-seeking sex story, for his downfall, but in truth he had dug a pit for himself and jumped into it.

Given the extent of these unhappy media experiences for England captains, it is surprising that Michael Atherton was the first to be sent, by the Test and County Cricket Board, on a course in media relations. He went, prior to handling his first overseas tour in charge, to the West Indies in early 1994, and he confirms he learned a lot from it – even though there have been times, especially during England's abysmal World Cup campaign of 1996, when that was not evident, as his wariness bordered on churlishness. In Australia, they go further. A firm of consultants is retained on permanent call by the Australian Cricket Board to advise and counsel players on handling themselves as public figures. This makes eminently good sense in an age in which the average cricketer is still ill-equipped to cope in the ever-expanding jungle of media expectations.

Dominic Cork fell into this category when, in the summer of 1995, he began his England career as remarkably as anyone in the game's history. He looks back on his reaction to his Test-winning spell against West Indies at Lord's on his debut, and accepts that he was unprepared.

> I have always enjoyed talking to the press and got along well with them, but this was something different. I had to drive straight from Lord's to a ground in March, Cambridgeshire, to play a NatWest Trophy game and it seemed that those of the press corps who did not follow me there were constantly on the pavilion telephone all through the following day. It was a very difficult time. I found it hard, almost impossible, to concentrate on the cricket and I counted thirty-two different interviews I gave during the day, all saying basically the same thing.
>
> When I finally got home to Derbyshire that night

there were five reporters outside my house. I phoned my mum and she said there was another group waiting at her gate and that all they wanted to know was whether I'd been a good boy at school. Mum had to leave her home for a couple of days, just to get away from it all. It felt intrusive and I didn't like it much. The press can help you as a player and certainly they can influence selection matters, but I find it annoying when people in sport are hounded in the hunt for sensational stories. I decided that night that I must get myself a decent agent.

And that, as we shall see, is another story.

12

Cash and Corruption

Midway through the century, the young cricketer who made headlines on his England debut would have had modest expectations of their effect on his life. There would be the cosy newspaper photographs of the new star at home, of course, perhaps with a proud mother brewing up a celebratory pot of tea behind him, and there would be the laddish shots of him enjoying a pint with his team-mates after play. Somebody would interview him on the radio, quite possibly somebody with plummy BBC vowels quite at odds with the self-conscious earthiness of the player, and for a day or two he might be recognized by a few eagle-eyed followers in the streets of his home town. He would be clapped on the back by well-wishers, sycophants and bores and given unsolicited and probably useless advice. After that, life would return pretty much to normal and, unless he was very lucky, the dramatic debut would not even have made him any money. The cricketer in the same situation today is in a very different position. His first move, almost as soon as he rubs the euphoria from his eyes, is to engage a manager to handle his affairs.

This trend has been greeted with much suspicion and resentment, and to decry all agents as rapacious scavengers, preying on the game for personal gain, is a natural enough knee-jerk reaction in the many who deplore the unstoppable spread of commercialism in cricket. Examples abound to support this jaundiced view, too, but this is to be unfair to certain agents, as well as to a number of players who have genuine need of them: Dominic Cork for one. When Cork decided after a single Test match, albeit a staggeringly successful one, that he would require an expert hand on the tiller of his finances, he was not being overtly mercenary, not even especially presumptuous. Given the facts of life of the cricketing meteor in the 1990s, a category to which he was confident enough to feel a sense of belonging, he was being eminently sensible, not least in his choice of manager.

Cork added his name to the glittering and sophisticated client list of Jon Holmes, already responsible for the commercial interests of such sporting smoothies as Gary Lineker, Will Carling and David Gower, as well as for Cork's England captain, Michael Atherton. Holmes' reputation is based on his consistency in achieving the ideals of the respectable agent: to protect and enhance the image of his players and their sport while making them tolerably rich from it. He carefully steers clear of potentially grubby deals and has a well-honed disrespect for the bottom end of the newspaper market, notwithstanding the chequebooks they have often waved in his direction in expectant exchange for sensational headlines concerning one or other of his flock. Certain of his competitors (he might not relish their being called colleagues) in the commercial jungle, men Cork was wise enough to reject, do not hold such principles in high regard.

Within a few months of their association being confirmed, it was clear that Cork and Holmes had been good for each other. Cork was young, trendily smart and confidently lucid and his natural marketability soared still further following his hat-trick against West Indies at Old Trafford in his third Test. He was bombarded with offers, some more genuine and more appealing than others. With Holmes' guidance, and sometimes through his instigation, he accepted a deal for a commercial for Pepsi-Cola, signed a contract for an immediate book on his remarkable year and even gripped the nation by appearing on the Saturday-evening National Lottery TV show to present a cheque. Simultaneously, a number of approaches were rebuffed. 'We just had to decide what was right for me and what wasn't,' explained Cork. 'My generation of England cricketers has a chance to make ourselves financially secure, but it is important to go about it in the right way.'

Cork's generation is, indeed, the first with the capability of making themselves rich. Until now, cricket had provided dreams, heroes, occasional glamour and an elegance sustained even against the onset of market forces, but it had not been an access route to the gravy train – not unless you were that freak whose charisma and ability would command wealth and fame in any generation, a freak like Denis Compton or Ian Botham. Compton, of course, was among the first cricketers to be used in commercial advertising – certainly the first to make an impact at it – and his Brylcreem advert was a classic of its time. He engaged an agent, the London-based Bagenal Harvey, and late in his career he enjoyed such trappings as ghosted books and newspaper columns. Doubtless he earned enough from such peripheral activities to afford his peers a twinge of envy but Compton, who possessed the rare but happy combination of abundant talent and companionability, was hugely popular and few will have begrudged him his deserts. Even fewer can seriously have believed he was making more from the game than he had put into it, for cricket's pot of gold was simply not that large.

Even a generation and more later, when the 1980s' reincarnation of Compton came to power in the form of Botham, the rewards available for cricketers were scant in comparison with their equivalents in other sports. Indeed, in his 1990 book *Sportsbiz*, the author Stephen Aris was briskly dismissive of cricket's place in his theme. 'Cricket remains a cottage industry,' he scoffed. 'Most of the £10 million a year that comes from sponsorship and TV is spent propping up the near-bankrupt counties.' Depressingly, Aris was right; or at least was right historically. By the time he wrote his book, the game had passed through its civil war, the years of world series cricket, and emerged, a decade later, battered, barely recognizable in some areas but undeniably wealthier.

Nick Faldo, whose eminence in his chosen sport could be realistically compared with that of Botham, won the Open Golf Championship in 1987. In the same year, Botham became the highest wicket-taker in the history of Test cricket and the first man ever to achieve the astonishing Test match double of 5,000 runs and 350 wickets (Sir Gary Sobers, by comparison, scored more than 8,000 runs but took only 235 wickets). Botham, though in the autumnal years of his playing career, was probably at the peak of his earning power and nobody could say he had to go short. Nevertheless, the revenue he attracted from endorsements, equipment deals, breakfast-cereal adverts and newspaper columns could not begin to rival that of Faldo. During 1988, cashing in on his Open win, Faldo charged £40,000 appearance money whenever he played in tournaments other than the majors; he received £330,000 for wearing those distinctively homely Pringle sweaters and £165,000 for using Wilson clubs. His business affairs were run by Mark McCormack's IMG company, who presented him with an off-course profit for the year of £1.5 million. Botham would have done well if he earned a tenth of that from his own commercial activities.

The fact is that money has always been something of a dirty word in cricket, especially money that might find its way to the players. Among the traditional figures who ran the game for so long there was a proprietorial air, not to mention a Dickensian belief, seldom voiced but always prevalent, that the cricketers themselves were hired hands, to be kept in their place on the shop floor. The rise of the players' representative body, the Professional Cricketers' Association, has eroded many of these primitive philosophies and their belated but welcome appointment of a full-time general secretary, David Graveney, in 1995 presaged a period of proactive negotiation with the employers, which is gradually improving the lot of the more junior players as well as the insurance and pension provisions for all. These, however, though welcome advances, were minor concessions to the altered times. The first-class cricketer in England continued to speak in relatively small figures; it was only those who aspired to higher honours for whom the financial barriers were down.

Tony Greig would claim a degree of credit for this. It has always been his contention that the cricketers of the current generation are reaping the rewards created by the Packer years. While even Greig might stop short of portraying himself as a martyr who gave up his inheritance (the England captaincy) for the good of his fellow player, there is some truth in what he says. When, in 1980, the minimum wage for capped county cricketers scaled the dizzy heights of £5,000, Greig pointed out: 'That is more than I was paid [by Sussex] when I was captain of England.'

But many will argue that the benefits of the Packer affair are not justified by the years of bitterness and division. Others will question whether anything can be considered beneficial within the legacy of that monumental dispute, sparked, as is so much within modern sport, by a contest over the rights to televise. Packer got his way, as was always likely considering the artillery of financial and legal expertise at his disposal, and his television station has continued to cover all international cricket in Australia ever since. But by demonstrating, to put it in its crudest sense, that the cricketer could be bought, that even the noblest of games was not immune to the corrupting influence of money, he was, to the most reactionary of minds, colluding with the Devil. Even those, like myself, who believed that such accelerated evolution was inevitable, that players deserved better rewards and that the game required an injection of modernism to retain and improve its place on the increasingly uncivil stage of sporting competition, could not and still cannot approve of all Packer's legacies, for he has eroded too much that was precious and replaced it with a single-minded pursuit of personal gain.

For the past two decades, within cricket, there has been plenty of incandescence on this issue, the purple-faced wrath of those who believe their game has been brutalized and that Packer and his cohorts are entirely to blame. Jack Fingleton was not of this persuasion, for he was seldom incandescent about anything, but the wise and educated Australian opening batsman who brought to journalism the same forthrightness he had brought to his batting, was nevertheless firmly in the anti-Packer camp. Two years before his death in 1981, Fingleton wrote: 'Cricket as I have known and admired it has gone . . . It is the day – and night – of the big buck.' Turning to Packer and the players who signed for him, he added: 'I can't help but think he and they have done the real game of cricket a great harm. It will never be the same.'

The same theme, that of money as a corrupting influence, was explored by Bob Taylor when he reflected on the legacy of the Packer era and bemoaned the fact that it had stripped the international game of its 'precious element of novelty'. His point was that the sense of occasion, that feeling of electric anticipation we can all conjure up from the time when every new series, every new Test match, was genuinely special, had been sacrificed on the altar of greed. 'The mystique has gone because we have to play so many Tests nowadays,' said Taylor. 'Money is so plentiful . . . When there is a stack of money available, human nature dictates that you grab at it, even when the ability that rocketed you to that eminence sometimes lets you down. World series cricket put us all on such a treadmill, and it became a test of character to cope with it.'

It was not, however, exclusively the upwardly mobile cricketers, those with a business brain and a keenly defined sense of their own self-importance, who were beguiled by the Packer project. Of the English players who signed up during those hectic weeks of subterfuge early in 1977, one could never imagine Derek Underwood as a mercenary with eyes only for the chequebook, or accuse Alan Knott of being a man with no finer feelings for his game. These were cricketers who might have fitted happily into more romantic ages, years when the sight of a left-arm spin bowler and his wicketkeeper in flawless concert on a hazardous pitch was enough for any aficionado. And yet they signed up, willingly enough, and were subsequently to be so taken by the treatment they received and the new directions in which the game was being pointed that they were greeted as converts by one side of the divide and derided as brainwashed by the other. Whatever the truth, the fact is they experienced something very different from their accustomed routine, something they believed to be good.

John Snow belonged to a different category. Unlike Underwood and Knott, who were respectively four and five years his junior and not subjected to the rigours of fast bowling, he was effectively at the end of his regular Test career and had more to gain than to lose by signing with World Series. Also, unlike the Kent pair, Snow had been a regular agitator on the question of the entitlement of cricketers to make money from the game and there had been occasions when his methods had not been well received by the establishment. For instance, in 1976, when Snow was recalled to the England side against West Indies to play, not without success, what turned out to be his final Test cricket, the issue of advertising logos on clothing was simmering. In Snow's view it had been simmering too long, placed deliberately on the back burner by a hierarchy which was philosophically opposed to the idea. Snow seldom backed away from any potential conflict with authority and he did not do so now: in a televised Sunday League game, he flagrantly wore a sponsor's logo on his flannels. Much hot air ensued from the Test and County Cricket Board and Snow was subsequently made a martyr (which was perhaps what he had sought all along) by a short suspension. What he had done, though, was to attract a wider attention on to an issue dear to his heart, an area in which he believed players were being unfairly deprived. Finally, though not without more procrastination, single logos were permitted.

This was one instance of what might be described as player power: change being brought about by the pre-emptive actions of a cricketer. Such examples have, however, been extremely rare, for cricket is a game that instinctively rebels against being hurried into change. It is a game that prefers gentle evolution and which, even now, has not come to terms with its true worth in the broader commercial marketplace. The dealings with sponsors and television have demonstrated this fact: until very recently, cricket was guilty of selling itself derisorily short, as much as anything, perhaps, through a long-standing discomfort when dealing with anything as tacky as money. Competition among television companies since the advent of satellite has something to do with this, of course, but even so, the disparity between the £1.5 million a year the English game was earning from television in the early 1990s and the £15 million a year which has been rolling in since the new agreement of 1994 is stark and revealing.

Sponsorship was admitted in the early 1960s, though at first with such inbred distaste that when Gillette backed the inaugural one-day competition in 1963 it was steadfastly referred to as 'the knock-out competition' throughout its first year. For years afterwards, many – perhaps even a majority – within the game regarded commercial sponsorship as a necessary evil rather than a mutually productive relationship, and realistic prices were not paid until . . . well, certainly until after Packer had awoken the game to the need for self-preservation. Cornhill Insurance, who mounted the rescue package for England's official Test cricket in the immediate aftermath of the

World Series sensations, was perhaps the first company to raise payments close to sensible levels, but even these were not commensurate with the phenomenal unseen benefits ('customer awareness', as companies call it) that they have gained from the association.

In itself, the question of sponsorship might appear to be unrelated to the lifestyle of the cricketers themselves, the spinal cord of this book. But it is not, because those lifestyles might have been substantially improved long before now if the people running the game had been more streetwise in negotiating deals with sponsors and television; and they might now be less harassed and subject to burn-out if those same people had not belatedly seen the commercial green light and responded by snatching at every offered crumb without the slightest thought for the damage it could cause future generations of players.

In a sense, it was through this disinclination to protect the welfare of the players in any calculated, long-term way that a window was created for the incursion of the percentage men, the agents. They would still have arrived, sooner or later, because the need for them as absorbents is greater now than ever before, but they need not and should not have been permitted to form and implement such a selective view of the leading players' requirements. Not everything about Australian and South African cricket is preferable to the English way, but their care for the players, especially for the national squad as a unit, is infinitely better. South Africa, having contracted all of their players and agreed their salary band, work on a give-and-take system in which the giving includes the provision of a manager to handle all the team's commercial interests and to advise them about image and responsibility. If such an appointment had been made in England some years ago, several disastrous liaisons between players who knew no better and managers whose sole interest was the annual bottom line from their 20 per cent could have been averted.

Raymond Illingworth was not of the generation to consort with agents. The closest he came to it was a working relationship with the admirable Reg Hayter, whose affiliations with a variety of footballers and cricketers generally extended little further than the acquisition of newspaper columns and book contracts. Illingworth, having brought out a ghosted 'autobiography' in 1969, had a newspaper column throughout the 1970s which covered a wide range of cricketing issues and was syndicated to a dozen or more provincial papers. I know all this because, for some years, I wrote it. There was nothing unusual about the Illingworth column, then or now, but what is striking about it, in hindsight, is that it provided one of the few additional sources of income to a man with as distinguished a reputation as any player of the time. And this, remember, was not more than twenty years ago.

Ian Botham was barging his way through the entrance halls of the game around this time, preparing the ground for a quite different level of earning power. He, too, had a business relationship with Reg Hayter, and a not unprofitable one to either side, but as Botham's fame grew, so did his ego. Reg's traditional methods were no longer adequate for him. Although Hayter broadened his commercial scope, delving into new areas, Botham always thought he was worth more. He forgot, or chose to overlook, that Hayter was worth far more to him than the percentage of his earnings he claimed; that Hayter had extricated him from an untold number of scraps and potentially damaging headlines by using his vast army of contacts to persuade and placate (again, I know because I was there and involved). Botham at this time was surrounded by the fawning hangers-on who plague all sportsmen whose excessive talent is combined with notoriety – I give you George Best, Paul Gascoigne and any number of professional boxers – and he was impressionable enough to take notice of them rather than heeding those who had his interests at heart. He allied himself with Tim Hudson, a relationship so farcical that it would require a separate book to do it justice (and then much thought as to whether it belonged in the category of humour or tragedy). Hudson dressed his client, and any other acolytes who wished to look foolish, in deck-chair-coloured blazers and convinced him he had a future in Hollywood. Unsurprisingly, Hollywood had a different view. Hudson also created his own cricket ground, on which Botham and other assorted stars of both the men's and women's game were enlisted to play Sunday games. But the pavilion was eventually put to another use − it became Hudson's home when his hollow promises had been exposed. Botham had left him in anger and remorse, and the money of which he had bragged was not in evidence. Thereafter, Botham employed a sequence of other managers. None lasted long, for whatever reasons of incompatibility. Botham there-fore ended his playing career without the money (although he was far from poor) or the peace of mind that he might have attained had he chosen his business acquaintances more carefully.

No one else of his generation had Botham's earning power, not even David Gower, but the players of the millennium will, and for them, the need to guard against both greed and manipulation will be acute. The money now washing around cricket, both through official channels and on the periphery, is immense, and no one can doubt its potential for corruption since the scandal over Australian players alleging that they were offered bribes to throw a match. Whatever else may be said about them, such accusations reflect on the intensity of the illegal betting market, concentrated mainly in Bombay, where phenomenal sums are wagered on cricket games by professional gamblers who do not like to lose. The existence of liaisons between such gamblers and leading players has never been proved, but the risk of such abuses is obvious and unsett-ling. Indeed before the 1996 World Cup, Australian players seriously considered withdrawal, with all its ramifications, when they received letters threatening to maim them, or worse.

Given the sums now available within cricket – and here I refer entirely to legally acquired sums – there is a theory that the benefit, the traditional reward of loyalty and longevity, is no longer appropriate. Indeed, it could be thought obscene that an international cricketer already earning close to £100,000 in a calendar year should be encouraged to augment that figure with a year-long orgy of dinners, auctions and loosely disguised commercial fund-raising – twelve months brandishing the begging bowl.

Micky Stewart, who had a long playing career with Surrey and England before his son, Alec, followed in his footsteps, is said to have remarked after a recent benefit dinner that Alec made more in a single night than he ever did in an entire season. As Stewart Junior declared around £250,000 from his benefit, it could equally be said that he made more in a single year than did his father in an entire career. That amount was rivalled by Graham Gooch's second benefit, or testimonial, in 1995, and it is regrettably true that in most cases the profile of the player dictates the relative success of the benefit. It should not be this way; it was never intended that it should be so, for the benefit was designed to take account not of a player's fame but of his having accomplished long service with relatively modest income. Many cricketers of the workaday type, no longer ambitious in international terms but plying an honest trade in the county game, have been sustained by the lure of the benefit after ten years as a capped player.

At first, the year comprised few events outside the traditional benefit match, so the ultimate case of misfortune must be that of Bertie Buse of Somerset who, in 1950, elected to take the championship fixture against Lancashire for his benefit game, only for it to end inside a day in an innings defeat. But Buse, more than Gooch or Stewart, was surely the type of player for whom the benefit year was devised and, as it has outgrown its conception and its purpose, with cricketers spreading their wings into unconnected areas and sometimes with quite unsuitable events, the abiding surprise about it is that the income remains untouched by tax.

Modern benefits are sophisticated affairs and, like most other monetary matters relating to the players, are generally handed over to the administration of others. As Richard Hutton wrote in a recent issue of the *Cricketer* magazine:

> The modern benefit has declined in its relevance to cricket and is now a high-profile business operated by expert fund-raisers and owing all its paternalism to the Inland Revenue. Punters willingly cough up £100 a head for a candlelit dinner in the Long Room at Lord's. An auction of cricket merchandise at a gala dinner can raise a five-figure sum. When a Lloyd's insurance person can be persuaded to compound his losses by paying at auction £6,000 for a shirt which Brian Lara was purported to have worn during his 375 not out, it has become money for old shirts.

Hutton also offered the benefit as one persuasive reason why English cricket carries so much 'dead wood' in the form of players who ought to have been pensioned off long ago. These players will often occupy a place on a county staff that could more usefully have been given to a young cricketer of potential, but clubs are understandably squeamish about disposing of old servants without the traditional sop, the hand-out. It has become a discredited system; there has to be a better way.

Gooch, for one, believes that benefits will gradually decrease in number quite naturally through the erosion of the loyalty factor that, until now, has been such a feature of English first-class cricket. Interestingly, he blames the agents.

> Players are far more aware of money now because there is so much more of it about. It is an incentive

to them in a way it never was to me in my early days. They want to know what other players are getting, and why. Then they want to make sure they are getting more. Agents now come to players and tell them they can get them a good deal at a different club. It happens in football and it is beginning to happen in cricket. So loyalty is being constantly undermined by the lure of the chequebook. The obvious outcome is that far fewer players will be completing their careers with one club.

Perhaps this is no bad thing. Perhaps the game in England would prosper with the stimulus of an open transfer market. But I doubt it. Certain players would become wealthier and certain clubs would begin to dominate to an unhealthy extreme. But the pockets being most handsomely lined would be those of the agents, whose influence on the game now entering sensitive years of disposable wealth needs no further encouragement.

13

The Next Generation

Cricket, rushing towards the millennium in overwrought fashion, does not lend itself to the crystal-ball treatment. It is moving too fast, changing too dramatically, so that considered predictions of the player's lifestyle in, say, the year 2016 will almost certainly be too sober and staid. For evidence of this, cast your mind back a generation to the mid-1970s, when England still quaintly went abroad as MCC; players, unaware of the designer possibilities in store, still wore white at all times; the West Indies still bowled bouncers in moderation and consequently helmets had not even reached the much-mocked experimental stage; one-day internationals were in their infancy, and no one was quite sure if it was worth persevering with them; and television, long before the onset of satellite, though only just before the unsubtle, jackbooted arrival of Kerry Packer, was subservient in its coverage of the game and negligible in its benefaction. A single generation has altered the game's pace and shape, overturned its traditional masters, outlook and audience. Who is to say that this turbulent process will not repeat itself, though in a different, currently unforeseeable form, as the new century dawns?

What can be said with confidence is that, two decades from now, cricket will be ever more a young man's game. Just as football's macho, dynamic modernism no longer sustains the

romantic notion of a latter-day Stanley Matthews still twink-
ling down the right wing when ten years short of his pension
book and bus pass, so cricket will soon have no place for the
Phyllosan brigade. This will be no bad thing in some respects,
especially in England, where the first-class structure has har-
boured far too many has-beens and quite a few never-weres,
but it will be a shock to many, nevertheless. There could,
after all, be no more fundamental a change in lifestyle than a
reduction in the length of an expected working life. English
cricketers, used to thinking in terms of a twenty-year career
extending to their late thirties – and in many cases well into
their forties – will instead have to make the best use of a dozen
years in the game. The pace of life at the top will not physically
or mentally permit the leading players to stay longer, while
the also-rans who have in times past made up the numbers in
what is now an unwieldy, unworkable English system will be
pruned.

If playing careers are to be shorter, however, they are also to
be considerably richer. Ask a contemporary player, a Dominic
Cork or a Darren Gough, how he expects cricket to change
during his career, and he will give a knee-jerk answer: 'There
will be more money available.' This is human nature speaking,
the jealous nag at the back of every mind that suspects the
next man in will have it easier than you. In one way, the
strictly financial way, this is sure to be true, for if cricket is
not rich in direct comparison with other professional games,
such as football, golf and tennis, it is awash with money compared to a generation ago. Some of the money, if inevitably
not as much as the players think they deserve, will gravitate
to the workforce.

Indeed, this process has already begun and Cork is the
English role model. Barely six months after making his Test
debut his life had changed bewilderingly. 'We can move into
our dream house,' he said proudly, speaking of his family, his
wife, Jane, and one-year-old-son, Gregory. 'And I have money

to invest, money I could not have considered before.' It sounds like a dewy-eyed television commercial for winning the football pools but, in Cork's case, and that of all others who aspire to his level in years to come, there will be penances to fame and fortune, penances that some will undoubtedly consider unreasonable.

Two problems will immediately confront the next generation of stars, problems that are not exactly new but will now be exaggerated. One is the age-old amalgam of muck and brass, the certainty that escalating wealth will bring with it a breeding ground for sharks, those opportunists and predators whose self-styled role as managers and promoters hides, in many cases, a ruthless and unprincipled nature and the simple aim of getting rich through someone else's talent. Then there is what the Australians call the tall-poppy syndrome, the unattractive trait that lurks within most of us and manifests itself in a desire to cut down the stems that flourish excessively – in other words, the star players – to a less imposing size. This will occur in all public places and especially in public forums such as tabloid newspapers, whose speciality in life is to promote and inflate an individual to an exalted level and then doltishly bring him down. Cricketers remain, in general, unworldly about such things, sensitive and impressionable when the cruder periscopes rise from the gutter to peer at their lives and make judgements upon them. Thicker skins will be required, because there is no sign of a slackening in the public support of the tabloids, nor, consequently, any softening of their approach. Periodical censure may come the tabloids' way when they become over-zealous in their assistance in the royal family's attempts to rival the storylines of *EastEnders*, but, in the tabloid mentality, sportsmen fall into the same category as politicians – that of public figures who can have no private lives. The intrusions are harsh, penetrative, often hurtful and sometimes unforgivable. But they will not go away.

It is in areas such as these that the players of tomorrow may need the kind of help that a financial manager cannot give but a psychologist can. Cricket, or at least English cricket, has been reluctant to acknowledge that the coaching of the modern player should not begin and end with the techniques of batting and bowling. Raymond Illingworth has been as guilty as any in this regard, despite an oft-repeated comment that cricket is played 'ninety per cent in the mind and bugger technique'. As England's omnipotent chairman and manager, he has paid no more than lip-service to his own view and has demonstrated a Yorkshireman's native disdain for the idea that players could benefit from counselling from those qualified in no kind of game other than mind games. Embraced with enthusiasm in other countries, sports psychology has continued to carry a taboo in English cricket, but this will change. The pressures on the leading players are now of an altogether differ-ent and more intense nature than they were when Illingworth played and, as management evolves in the coming years, there will be a swift and unquestioning acceptance that the players require experts to help them cope. Mark Ramprakash is one prominent English player who has already taken matters into his own hands. He enlisted the help of the former England captain Mike Brearley, now a practising psychotherapist, when his Test career appeared to be suffering from chronic lack of confidence. Other individuals have pursued similar courses, as have a few teams. The England women's team, which won their version of the World Cup in 1993, employed a sports psychologist. Thus far, their male equivalents have resisted.

The direction of cricket management itself is more unclear. Some teams will continue to prefer a technical coach as an adjunct to the captain, while others will pursue the option of a more authoritarian, motivational off-field figure who, as Illingworth has been prone to do, may sometimes usurp the captain. Certainly, there will be more management figures, both at Test and first-class level, and their means of transmitting information will become more sophisticated. England are only just accustoming their senses to the regular use of videos; heaven knows what computerized aids will be employed in the preparation of teams in twenty years' time. It is far from impossible that players will wear earpieces wired up to their manager on the balcony, who will issue instructions, as already happens in that perennially baffling game of American football. Heaven forbid.

Technology cannot now be turned back and rejected, even in such an intrinsically reactionary game as cricket. One can only hope and trust that it will be handled sensitively, not with the crass indiscretion that has already prevailed in some parts of the world, where the aim has apparently been to turn a game – specifically a floodlit one-day game – into a computer fairground. It is one thing to impose black sightscreens on the game as an antidote to the white ball; it is quite another to use it as an electronic advertisement hoarding. Ted Dexter once told me that one of his great regrets about cricket in the 1990s was the aesthetic vandalism that is perimeter advertising. 'I am lucky enough to be an honorary member of MCC, but I would gladly pay £100 a year if Lord's could be freed of the hoardings,' he said. What, I wonder, can Dexter make of the animated electronic scoreboard, barely pausing to fulfil its official function at the end of each over before darting off into the commercial world of the area; or of the sightscreen which, when the machinery develops a flaw, can remain stuck on its endorsement of the local chicken take-away while the fast bowler is pawing the ground at the end of his run-up and the umpire is performing agitated gyrations at the 'control tower' which was once a mere score box.

Ah, the umpires. How their lives have changed within a generation, and how they are sure to change again, for in their sphere of operations technology has taken a hold. Was it this that prompted the unheralded retirement of Harold 'Dickie' Bird early in 1996? Assuredly Bird's wings had been clipped by the advent of a third umpire for major games and the consequent demand for all tight line decisions to be referred for adjudication by the hidden eye. It did not suit his style, had no place within his view of cricket as a human game, where all fallibilities are acceptable and all disputes can be repaired by sensible relations. Such ideals are now scorned as old-fashioned, which is a dreadful shame, and the reason is the twin-track, orchestrated advance upon cricket of television and money. In the coming years, the intertwining of the two will have more impact upon players than any other factor.

Television rights – the entitlement, exclusive or shared, to cover cricket series and competitions – is a perennial sore upon the game around the world. When amicably resolved, as was quite wondrously achieved by the Test and County Cricket Board's sub-committee in England in 1994, the rights issue can be hugely beneficial for the game itself, but there is always a next time, always the possibility that the juggling act between channels, and increasingly between terrestrial and satellite media, will prove impossible. When this occurred in Australia a generation ago, and the authorities declined the highest bid to keep faith with their traditional television relationship, Kerry Packer decided that if he could not buy cricket from the official vendors he would buy it through the players themselves. His audacious recruitment of a majority of the leading players of the world was a form of hijacking, holding the game to ransom. Reprehensible, no doubt, within the accepted morals of sport and its business dealings, but not so unusual in the wider world of commerce. The tactics used by Packer, vilified though he was, proved successful on two levels: he was vindicated in a court of law and he ultimately gained the rights to show Australian cricket on Channel 9, which was the genesis of the whole affair. Among all the hot air and indignation that has since been expended on the matter, the most pertinent point is that it could easily happen again, and the players of the millennium are more vulnerable than any of their predecessors.

Here is a potential scenario. The existing round of television rights for English cricket extend to 1999 and negotiations will resume long before their expiry with a view to establishing an arrangement for the new century. There is a major snag in the shape of the perceived political correctness of preserving the major sporting events – the institutions – for the nation rather than the minority who own a satellite dish. Test cricket in England is a listed event, like Wimbledon, the FA Cup final and the Derby, so that at present it cannot be sold to satellite TV. Cricket, in the shape of the Test and County Cricket Board, is righteously resentful about this, arguing that a Test series is potentially 180 hours of live sport, as against the two minutes it takes to run the Derby; they are pleading that it is unfair on these grounds and could be hugely damaging to a sport only now reaping the benefits of competition for TV rights. They may win their case, but if they do not, if the government of the day persists with the view that only a terrestrial channel – in this case, inevitably, the BBC – can cover Test cricket, two things will happen. The BBC will bid a relative pittance when the rights are renegotiated, knowing that their opposition is negligible, and Sky TV will brood about the injustice of it. Thus far, Sky have been happy to show overseas series, concentrating in the summer on one-day cricket, Test highlights and regular magazine programmes. They will not be so easily pleased in future. Sky, for the unaware, is owned by Rupert Murdoch, whose power and influence is at least the equal of Kerry Packer's; Murdoch has already moved in to revolutionize rugby league on both sides of the globe and, if the fancy takes him, if his pride is hurt by a door slammed in his face, he could do the same to cricket.

Murdoch, deprived of official Test cricket in England, could create his own game, his own teams. With the virtually limit-less depths of his chequebook he could undoubtedly seduce sufficient high-quality players to stage something similar in concept, if not in ultimate shape, to world series cricket. Certainly, if he concentrated on English-based players and the northern-hemisphere summer, he could not only undermine the official England Test team, whose stars would find it difficult to remain loyal against such courtship, but also destroy county cricket as we know it.

There will be players who consider such a venture exciting; undoubtedly it would be lucrative. But it would also be short-term, probably for as long as it took the concerned parties to back down and allow Sky to cover international cricket. Then the English game would have to pick itself up and put the pieces together, just as Australia did post-Packer. Some good, and plenty of bitterness and scars, would result.

That is a worst-case scenario. Much more attractive, and, it is to be hoped, more probable, is a situation whereby the game takes control of its own destiny, TV rights notwithstanding, and creates a product that is irresistibly authentic – something no Packer or Murdoch-inspired circuit could ever truly be. Cricket lags behind the professional sporting world in the creation of a genuine international competition, within which champions can be identified and crowned on a regular basis. It has a World Cup every four years, but this is a fraudulent exercise so far as establishing supremacy is concerned, for it involves only limited-overs cricket, with all its attendant imponderables. In 1996, when Sri Lanka were the surprising but thoroughly deserving winners, it was also little more than an obscenely single-minded exercise in money-making. The winners of the World Cup are not the world champions of cricket, simply of the fast-food version. What is needed is a Test match championship, a league system in which the countries, currently free to organize their fixture lists with as much discretion and prejudice as a village side, play to an itinerary prescribed for them from a central office.

At present there are only nine Test-playing countries. This is insufficient, especially as Zimbabwe are not genuinely up to standard. The aim, and one which is cherished by such enlightened men as Ali Bacher in South Africa and David Richards, the Australian at the executive helm of the International Cricket Council, must be to increase this number, initially to twelve and then to sixteen. Even with twelve teams, one could structure a league system for Test matches, perhaps in two divisions, which would create enormous interest and improve incalculably upon potential revenue. To me, the only surprise is that the late 1990s have been reached and still there are no serious moves to activate such a scheme. This, though, is the fault of the game's traditional leaning towards a disparate democracy in which countries meet periodically to debate the game's issues but then disperse and do their own favoured thing, leaving the notional management body (the ICC) waving limply from the sidelines. Until proper executive decisions are made, until power is put in the hands of elected individuals whose talent is action rather than warm words, the game will be missing its destiny.

There will be cries around the shires that such a development would further promote international cricket at the expense of the counties. Of course it would. That is the way the game must head, even in England. We must never abandon county cricket, nor lose sight of the fact that it does have functions other than its role as a nursery for the Test team, an abiding appeal and a comfortingly measured tread through each summer that internationals cannot hope to rival. But perhaps if it was suitably streamlined, the one-day events reduced from three to a maximum of two and the championship games scheduled so that they are an occasion rather than an encumbrance, it could prosper alone, rather than being constantly propped up by Test match revenue. Whatever its future, it is the national team which will increasingly dominate the popular focus of the game. Twenty years from now it is possible that the leading cricketers, once they have graduated from county level and played for England, will not return to the domestic structure at all, instead operating exclusively on the international circuit for as long as their England career lasts. Players would retain their county affiliations, so that they could naturally drop down a grade if they needed to recover from injury or lack of form, but while their place in an England squad remained, they would be contracted to a central board and paid by England. It is not such a phenomenal step as such a system already operates, in effect, in other countries. The plain fact is that it is now a full-time occupation to play cricket for England. The duties are not about to get any lighter.

Much more of a less fundamental nature will happen to the twenty-first century cricketer. He may travel between matches in private jets, stay in country clubs owned by the game, appear in commercials advertising the latest offshoot of his employers' (the English Cricket Board) business. He will wear different clothes, adopt different accessories to replace or augment the helmets, sunglasses and sunblock of the 1990s. He will invent variations on technique, he will engage in ever more sessions of bonding, motivation and mental strength, consult an ever-increasing army of experts. He will be paid well and he will be subjected to temptations to behave badly. Those who do not, those who become acceptable role models for an audience that may be further polarized by the broadsheet and tabloid of Test and one-day cricket, will be rich beyond the conception of the cricketers of fifty years ago. But then, the lives of those players, those of Raymond Illingworth's era and before, cannot with relevance be compared to the cricketers of the twenty-first century. They were playing a different game.

Bibliography

Agnew, Jonathan, *8 Days a Week* (Ringpress, 1988)

Botham, Ian, *Botham* (Collins Willow, 1994)

Fletcher, Keith, *Captain's Innings* (Stanley Paul, 1983)

Fry, C. B., *Life Worth Living* (Pavilion, 1986)

Gooch, Graham, and Frank Keating, *Gooch, My Autobiography* (Collins Willow, 1995)

Illingworth, Ray, *Spinner's Wicket* (Stanley Paul, 1969)

Lever, J. K., and Pat Gibson, *A Cricketer's Cricketer* (Unwin Hyman, 1989)

Richards, Barry, *The Barry Richards Story* (Faber, 1978)

Simmons, Jack, *Flat Jack* (Queen Anne Press, 1986)

Snow, John, *Cricket Rebel* (Hamlyn, 1976)

Taylor, Bob, *Standing Up, Standing Back* (Collins Willow, 1985)

Willis, Bob, *Lasting the Pace* (Collins Willow, 1985)

Index